Praise for *Decision Intelligence*

"In *Decision Intelligence*, Thorsten Heilig and Ilhan Scheer build a compelling case for the world of tomorrow's version of decision-making."

—Martin Lindstrom
New York Times best-selling author

"Decision Intelligence will be one of the big topics for this decade and completely change the way organizations manage, plan, and operate. This book provides a comprehensive guide from the basics to the applications."

—Niklas Jansen
Entrepreneur and Tech Investor,
Founding Partner Interface Capital and
Co-Founder Blinkist

"The book impressively demonstrates the potential and entry points into the world of AI-powered decision making. A very valuable reading for managers and their organizations."

—Michael Kleinemeier
Member of the Merck KG Board of Partners,
former Member of the SAP SE Executive Board

"The AI hype perfectly captured, easy to understand, de-mystified, and mapped to clear use cases. A must-read for today's managers."

—Dr. Daniela Gerd tom Markotten
Member of the Management Board for Digitalization
and Technology, Deutsche Bahn AG

"Artificial Intelligence can help leaders make better decisions and is thus crucial to maintain competitive edge. Thorsten and Ilhan tangibly describe the fundamentals of Decision Intelligence and how to practically apply it to your business as well as how to healthily balance the human-machine interactions. An indispensable read!"

—Florian Reuter
former CEO of Volocopter,
World Economic Forum Technology Pioneer

"Smart decisions are equally crucial in poker and in organizations! The concepts discussed in this book are the exciting approach to bring together human intuition and state-of-the-art AI and Machine Learning to make better decisions within companies and teams."

—Fedor Holz
Entrepreneur and 2x Poker World Champion

"For the very first time, an unprecedented era of artificial intelligence has surpassed the domain of spellcheckers, chess, and facial recognition, attaining superhuman prowess in solving intricate real-world challenges. This book perfectly captures an important perspective on the most rapid Industrial Revolution to date, bearing both opportunities and profound responsibilities, not solely upon technologists, but shared among entrepreneurs, leaders, and experts across every discipline."

—Jonas Andrulis
Founder & CEO Aleph Alpha

"With its profound insights into Decision Intelligence, this book delivers a wealth of benefits to C-level executives, decision-makers, and students alike. A true source of inspiration, it illuminates the path to a future where data and AI-based forecasting intertwine, unlocking plenty of opportunities."

—Prof. Dr. Frauke Schleer-van Gellecom
Partner PwC

"*Decision Intelligence* gives future-shapers a good look at Artificial Intelligence and Data. The book shows how modern predictive analytics and human intuition form the basis for making decisions for a more complex world, taking people in the company along on this journey."

—Kay Schiebur
Group Executive Vice President Services
at the Otto Group

"On the back of the rapid development of IoT, 5G SA and hardware, entirely new opportunities for AI-driven innovation in organizations are emerging, as described in this book. It will create a new generation and level of unbeatable automated industrialization and intelligent and connected production cycles."

—Hannes Ametsreiter
former CEO Germany and Member of the Group
Executive Committee, Vodafone

"Decision Intelligence is currently one of the central topics in organizations worldwide to be prepared for the future. Finally, this mega-trend is also captured in a book in a compact, holistic, and entertaining way!"

—Heiko Kahrels
Partner Decision Intelligence,
EY Germany

"An easy read with a deep understanding of the various ways AI can be leveraged for modern organizations. Should be a must-read in board rooms, business classes and leadership programs."

—Christoph Burkhardt
Keynote Speaker, Author *Don't be a Robot*,
former CEO One Life, Founder Tiny Box

"In a world driven by data, our true compass remains human intuition. Embrace AI, but never let it overshadow the warmth of human understanding. This book describes in an extremely readable way how to bring these two worlds together."

—Ronald Van Loon
CEO Intelligent World,
Top10 AI-Data-IoT-Influencer

"The greatest business transformation of our time—well summarized in one book and, above all, presented and distilled into an applicable format for companies. Clear reading recommendation for startups to large corporations!"

—Andreas Unseld
Tech Investor, General Partner UVC

"Most AI technologies are known for over 30 years but their application is still limited. This tangible book provides the missing ingredients to close the gap between technology and human decision making to unlock the full potential of AI."

—Fabian Rang
Cofounder & CTO paretos

Decision Intelligence

THORSTEN HEILIG ILHAN SCHEER

Decision Intelligence

TRANSFORM YOUR TEAM AND ORGANIZATION WITH AI-DRIVEN DECISION-MAKING

WILEY

Published by John Wiley & Sons, Inc., Hoboken, New Jersey.
Published simultaneously in Canada.

For general information on our other products and services or for technical support, please contact our Customer Care Department within the United States at (800) 762-2974, outside the United States at (317) 572-3993 or fax (317) 572-4002.

Wiley also publishes its books in a variety of electronic formats. Some content that appears in print may not be available in electronic formats. For more information about Wiley products, visit our web site at www.wiley.com.

Library of Congress Cataloging-in-Publication Data is Available:

ISBN 9781394185061 (cloth)
ISBN 9781394185443 (ePub)
ISBN 9781394185122 (ePDF)

Cover Design: Paul McCarthy

SKY10055240_091423

"Every single decision we make, every breath we draw, opens some doors and closes many others. Most of them we don't notice. Some we do."

—Douglas Adams

Contents

Figures List

Foreword

In the fast-paced, dynamic world of business, we are making decisions every second. As technology accelerates the pace of change, we find ourselves constantly responding to new information, new opportunities, and new challenges. Yet some of the world's best thinkers, philosophers, and business leaders – think Steve Jobs, for instance – have been known for taking long pauses, sometimes even up to 30 seconds, before sharing their responses. I remain convinced that, in all the rush, good decisions require reflection and intuition. Sound decisions emerge out from quiet reflections, from calm environments, and from conversations that allow many voices to be heard, to grow equally balanced thought patterns, and then make the call.

Consider this: we're often seduced by the promise of data, its ability to recount where we've been with unwavering certainty. It's alluring, isn't it? But let's step back for a moment and think about it. Can data, in its cold precision, truly illuminate where we are heading? Perhaps not.

Data, while valuable, is like a rearview mirror. It can perfectly detail the road traveled, but the path ahead? That's a different story. The future is uncharted territory, a journey not yet embarked upon, a tale not yet told.

In our quest to navigate the future, we mustn't lose sight of our uniquely human insight. It's our compass, our guiding star.

It transcends the reach of data, infusing our decisions with the warmth of human understanding, empathy, and intuition. These human elements shape not just the decisions we make but also the very fabric of our interactions. In a world bewitched by data, let's not forget our inherent human ability to dream, to imagine, and to create – to chart a course toward a future not yet seen. After all, isn't it these human insights that truly hold the power to tell us where the world is heading?

However, with the emergence of Decision Intelligence – a new discipline that courageously combines human intuition and artificial intelligence for strategic and operational planning – I do see a promising shift on the horizon. This book, *Decision Intelligence: Transform Your Team and Organization with AI-Driven Decision-Making*, by Thorsten Heilig and Ilhan Scheer, masterfully captures this evolution.

The book presents an approach that might indeed predict where the world is heading in our ever-changing business landscape. It advocates a balanced and nuanced way of decision-making that draws on both data and human insights. This dual-pronged approach could potentially revolutionize how we make decisions, bringing a level of foresight and strategic thinking previously unattainable.

Recently, when I spent time with the CEO of one of the leading FMCG (fast-moving consumer goods) companies in the US, I asked him how much time he spent by himself only – away from screens, his phone, and meeting rooms – just reflecting on the situation. He paused and was silent for nearly two minutes. Then he answered, "Right now is probably the longest time I've had in the past years thinking about a question." That very week, he reserved the first four hours of every Friday morning for what he called "thinking time."

Here's the issue: we rarely take the time to think deeply, and in a world where answers are expected not in hours but in minutes, we often share reactive rather than proactive thoughts. If this becomes part of our behavior, our routine, our brains adapt. We're suddenly no longer comfortable spending time alone, without a smartphone at the ready, or without hearing that constant string of dings signaling incoming emails – because it makes us feel like we've been disconnected. Useless, irrelevant. Out of tune. All while the world – with the latest version of ChatGPT – passes us by at breakneck speed.

Six years ago, I jumped into the ocean of silence. I got rid of my phone. Not just the smart version, but *every* version. Not an easy task given that I spent more than a million miles a year in the air, traveling across the globe. The week after the beginning of my detox, I experienced a sense of loneliness, emptiness, even despair – something akin to what an addict might feel as they do the hard and necessary work of going through withdrawal.

But over time, I felt my way of thinking change. My personal assistant told me I was much easier to deal with – not sending and resending the same orders repeatedly, as she expressed it. My clients even embraced the idea, at first thinking it was a joke, then realizing it might be a source of my creativity and balanced reflections.

These pauses help us to put things in perspective, change directions, reflect, and simulate scenarios that may at first seem trivial, but once pondered they often make a lot of sense. How can we possibly make any of these great calls if the speed of reply time is what is perceived as the KPI?

Time after time I've met great leaders out in the world, and many seem to have adopted pauses in their everyday lives – breaks in the busy daily calendar meant for intentional reflections. As ChatGPT seeps into every juncture of our lives and informs our decision-making, enabling us to craft essays, reflect on the most hardcore philosophical questions, or even conduct risk analysis in a matter of seconds, we'll all be tempted by the seduction it offers – making us more efficient, productive, perfect leaders and decision-makers – whereas one could easily argue that the exact opposite is the case.

In *Decision Intelligence*, Thorsten Heilig and Ilhan Scheer build a compelling case for the world of tomorrow's version of decision-making. It's a world representing tools unheard of just a year ago. Yet it's also a world where cultures are struggling to survive, where personal interactions are a thing of the past, where budgets are ever tighter, and where the legal implications have never been larger and the rewards smaller. The authors explore all of the potential wonders that AI brings to the table, the efficiencies that such technology offers, all while considering the flip side: the temptation to abuse it, the shortcuts, the assumptions, and the plain laziness.

This book is a delicately balanced cocktail – mixed up with knowledge, insight, and experience worth tapping into before you're tempted to assume that all AI tools are of highest caliber and quality.

Be warned that it will take you more than a few minutes to read the following pages. Asking ChatGPT, the chatbot informed me that it would take 262 minutes total. That's a lot if you evaluate things in terms of speed over quality. But if you believe that quality content – and time – is the most important asset of our day and age and a worthwhile investment for the future, well, it's really not that much at all. Especially since you are increasingly more likely to be dumped into another round of decision-making – where AI seems to be the first point on the agenda.

—Martin Lindstrom, *New York Times* best-selling author of *Buyology*, *Small Data*, and *The Ministry of Common Sense*

Acknowledgments

Sometimes life plays in strange coincidences. When we had the idea for the book three years ago, Decision Intelligence (DI) was still very small as a topic. Moreover, almost no one called it that. But then DI suddenly went through the roof, first in the bubble of digital and research companies, then in consulting. After OpenAI launched ChatGPT at the end of 2022, the notion of using AI for decision-making became widespread, even though ChatGPT itself is a bad decision for good decision-making. Nevertheless, it paved the way for incorporating AI into everyday applications.

Let's be honest: we always had the book on our list, but the project was "one of many." But then Wiley approached us, noticing the growing demand for Decision Intelligence. From minute one we shared the excitement for examining the topic from both a technological and a cultural standpoint. The journey of transforming organizations into DI organizations is a huge shift, and humans are still at the heart of it.

So, thanks to the Wiley teams in the US and in Europe (Sally, Annie, Deborah, Amy, Jutta, and many more) supporting us on our way so patiently.

Call us dreamers, but we thought of writing this book in the same way it began. We sit in cozy cafes and are immersed in thoughts and discussions. Then Captain Reality kicked in and reminded us that we are not full-time authors but have demanding leadership roles in our organization. This is why this book demanded everything from us and our surroundings.

We can assure you that without the people around us, helping, supporting, and pushing, this book would have never ended up in your hands.

So, a big, big thank you to:

Fabian Rang, cofounder and CTO of paretos, who was a substantial part of building the tech chapters – and also a great proofreader and discussion partner for every topic

Tina Sternberg, the "master of text and content," who was our stable pillar from the beginning, and while we were sometimes irritated by her asking for "which source, again?" ;) this really brought us to a next level here

Konrad Heimpel, for providing some more real-life use-cases for the "DI in practice"

Christoph Burkhardt and Magnus Haensler, who know how to write good books (for digital topics and for thriller novels) and supported us with good tips

Simon Kondermann, for the great sprint designing the illustrations

Ksenia Zheltoukhova, Alexander Schaper, Torin Monet, Dennis Nagel, and Enrico Ferro for the conversations, discussions, and challenging our thinking to bring this book to a new level of greatness

In addition, a big thank you to all the clients, investors, and other dialogue partners with whom we had discussions around the DI topic– it means a lot to us!

Last but definitely not least, we are really grateful for our private environment, which was so kind with us as we were writing and not being very social (especially at the end), and first and foremost we are grateful to our families (Jana, Elias, Leon, Lena, Oskar, Lotti, Juli) for being incredibly wonderful pillars and motivating us to make this possible!

Introduction

It was a warm day in Heidelberg, Germany, back in 2020, when we – Ilhan and Thorsten, two startup CEOs – found ourselves deep in conversation about our challenges. We were drinking a cappuccino and an Americano in Café Nomad, exchanging stories, experiences, and insights, coaching each other through the uncertainties ahead.

Ilhan, the founder of fable+, had successfully scaled the company over the years, transforming the way businesses approach team dynamics, data-driven change, and psychological safety with AI-driven decision engines. However, the unforeseen consequences of the COVID-19 pandemic introduced unpredictable and significant challenges to the consulting industry, which slowed the momentum of scaling.

Thorsten, on the other hand, had just come out of a corporate startup manager role with a suitcase full of exciting experiences. In light of the challenges he had seen, he was in the process of starting paretos, a pioneering company specializing in AI-fueled, data-driven decision-making (still rather an unknown field at the time), and faced the massive task of raising money for the new company against the backdrop of the pandemic. As we coached each other through the challenges of leadership, strategy, and decision-making, it became increasingly clear that Decision Intelligence was an area that warranted more attention, especially during these uncertain times. The ability to harness the power of data and human psychology to make informed decisions was a crucial skill for businesses navigating the rapidly changing landscape.

And so the idea for this book was born. We envisioned a comprehensive guide combining our unique expertise and experiences in Decision Intelligence, drawing from our respective backgrounds in psychological safety, team dynamics, data science, technology, and Pareto optimal optimization. Our goal was to empower leaders and organizations to make better decisions in the face of uncertainty and challenges, no matter how impossible they might seem. As the story unfolded, fable+ was successfully acquired by Accenture, paving the way for further growth and impact on a larger scale globally.[1] Meanwhile, despite the challenges of raising capital during a global crisis, paretos successfully secured relevant funding, enabling the company to pursue its mission of optimizing business performance through data-driven decision-making.

In this book, we share our collective knowledge, experiences, and insights on Decision Intelligence, drawing from our respective journeys as leaders and entrepreneurs. We delve into the art and science of making informed decisions, exploring the various tools and techniques that can be employed to navigate the complex world of business.

We examine the importance of psychological safety, team dynamics, and the second great theory of Pareto (besides the well-known 80/20 Pareto principle) in shaping the decision-making process while discussing the role of technology, data analytics, and behavioral science in enhancing Decision Intelligence. Through a combination of case studies, practical

[1]https://newsroom.accenture.com/news/accenture-acquires-fable-to-expand-capabilities-in-analytics-drivenand- workplace-cultures.htm

examples, and expert advice, we aim to equip you, our readers, with the necessary skills and knowledge to make better decisions for your organizations, even in the most challenging circumstances.

One of the key challenges we faced was balancing the human and data-driven aspects of decision-making. We wanted to ensure that the book provided a holistic approach to Decision Intelligence, considering the decision-making process's emotional, cognitive, and analytical dimensions. We also wanted to address the common pitfalls and biases hindering effective decision-making. To this end, we have included chapters on cognitive biases, and emotional intelligence, providing readers with a comprehensive toolkit to overcome these obstacles and make more informed decisions.

Another challenge was distilling the vast amount of research and information on decision-making into an accessible and engaging format. We aimed to create a book that was informative and enjoyable to read, with a narrative that would resonate with a wide range of readers, from seasoned executives to aspiring entrepreneurs. The topic of Decision Intelligence has been greatly hyped in the tech world lately – not least since the introduction of ChatGPT and the GPT models – and it is finally clear to everyone: the age of AI in application has started.

Now, three years after that day in the coffee shop, we have combined our personal stories and experiences with insights from industry experts, academic research, and real-world case studies. By sharing our experiences and expertise we hope to contribute to a future where leaders and organizations are better equipped to navigate uncertainty, embrace change, and make strategic decisions that drive growth, innovation, and long-term success. As the world continues to evolve at an ever-increasing pace, the importance of effective decision-making cannot be overstated.

We believe that this book will provide you with an entertaining and substantial contribution to transform your teams and your organization from data-centric to decision-centric. We are already looking forward to your comments and views (including – with pleasure – even the critical ones) that you might want to share with us.

Hopefully, our book will inspire you to become an advocate for Decision Intelligence and the Decision Intelligence organization within your own sphere of influence, sharing your newfound knowledge and insights with colleagues, peers, and partners. Let's change how we approach decision-making, embracing the power of data, psychology, and human-centered design to create a more sustainable, equitable, and prosperous future for all.

All the best,
Thorsten and Ilhan
Heidelberg, Germany
August 19, 2023

CHAPTER

1

Decoding Decision-Making: Good and Bad Decisions

"Every decision you make affects every facet of your life."

– Michael Jordan

Imagine sitting in a bustling café[1] in Heidelberg with us, sipping a cup of coffee, watching people come and go. Your gaze lands on someone by the window, deep in thought, brow furrowed as they ponder a decision. We have all been in these moments – the complexity and difficulty of a decision weighing heavy on us, feeling like we have to navigate a maze of choices, trying to find the right directions.

In this chapter, we'll embark on an intellectual journey exploring the nuances of good and bad decisions and why the dichotomy of right and wrong is oversimplified. We will explore the intricacies of human decision-making, learning from history's greatest thinkers and discovering how the past can inform our present choices.

Let's begin with a simple yet powerful question: What makes a decision good or bad? As it turns out, the answer is as complex as the decisions themselves. A decision's quality is not determined by a simple binary choice of right or wrong, but rather by the fine balance between the values at stake, the context, and the potential consequences. Recognizing this complexity frees us from the shackles of absolutes and empowers us to navigate the ever-shifting decision-making landscape.

To illustrate this point, consider two leaders tasked with addressing a looming crisis. One leader, focused on immediate relief, allocates resources to mitigate the short-term consequences. Meanwhile, the other leader adopts a long-term approach, investing in preventive measures to avoid a similar crisis in the future. Which decision is "right"? Well, the answer to that question depends on the values and priorities at play and

[1]If you ever have the opportunity to visit Heidelberg, make sure to stop by Café Nomad to enjoy the mix of historical small town and the new beat of the up-and-coming digital startup scene.

the unique circumstances of each scenario. Besides, one is always wiser afterward – thus decisions must always be evaluated in the light of the situation and the level of information available at the time they were made (see also Kahneman & Tversky, 1979). The thing about decision-making is that it often takes work to determine whether a decision is good or bad. Sometimes we only realize the consequences of our choices after some time. As the saying goes, "Hindsight is 20/20." In other words, we have a clearer understanding of the best course of action only after the dust has settled.

To quote American author and humorist Mark Twain, "Good decisions come from experience, and experience comes from bad decisions." This wisdom highlights that we often become more intelligent and better decision-makers by learning from the consequences of our previous choices. When reflecting on past decisions, it's essential to remember that what might seem like a wrong decision at the time could be a valuable learning experience that shapes our future choices.

Another question for the modern decision-maker is this: For whom is this decision good? And who stands to lose from this decision? Not only do decisions have to be taken in the context of the best strategy to reach a desired outcome, but they also might need to negotiate multiple contexts of the stakeholders – who may often be seeking competing outcomes. Moreover, this process is not simply about effective communication and compromise. Those involved in and affected by the decision will have unequal negotiating power, and it is the skill of the leader to recognize that and create a psychologically safe environment that surfaces all voices. (See, for example, Edmondson, 1999; because we consider psychological safety to be a crucial topic here, we have devoted Chapter 8 to it.) By embracing this mindset, we can better navigate the complexities of our world and make more informed choices that ultimately lead to better outcomes for all.

Decision-making is a fundamental aspect of management and involves choosing between different options based on available information and analysis. It is a process that requires the identification of a problem or opportunity, followed by the generation and evaluation of possible solutions. Ultimately, a decision is made based on the best available option, taking into account various factors such as risk, opportunity cost, and potential outcomes. In the context of business, a good decision is one that aligns with the organization's goals and values and has a positive impact on the company's financial and operational performance, as well as further key aspects and targets set by the organization, such as sustainability, social responsibility, and environmental aspects. A good business decision is also one that considers the interests of all stakeholders, including customers, employees, shareholders, and the community at large.

In addition, decision-making can be particularly challenging in today's fast-paced and hypercompetitive business world. While it is essential to acknowledge that mistakes are an inherent part of human behavior, they can also lead to bigger risks, sanctions, and failures. That being said, it is essential for organizations, individuals in leadership positions, and every employee to cultivate their decision-making skills to effectively navigate the constantly changing business landscape. As you explore this book further, you'll discover how Decision Intelligence can help you make better decisions by optimizing the use of information and cutting-edge predictive analytics (Chapter 6). Plus, you'll learn about the importance of fostering a mature data and decision culture (Chapter 7).

The transformation to a *Decision Intelligence organization* cultivates a culture of learning and improvement within organizations, encouraging individuals and groups to collaborate, experiment, and provide feedback (see also Chapter 8). This culture enables organizations to transform mistakes and failures into opportunities for growth and development. To effectively implement Decision Intelligence within an organization, certain prerequisites must be in place, including the necessary tools, processes, and culture. Organizations must create a culture that motivates individuals to invest their efforts and take interpersonal risks. This culture should foster experimentation, collaboration, and speaking up with ideas and concerns (Edmondson & Lei, 2014).

How to Measure the Quality of a Decision

Making a decision, especially one that influences the outcomes for numerous people, requires careful consideration and attentiveness to optimize decision quality (Gigerenzer & Selten, 2002). For example, imagine being in a position where your choices could shape the future of a large organization. In such situations, examining at least six major inputs contributing to a well-informed decision is crucial. Furthermore, since these inputs form the foundation of a complex decision, executing each as effectively as possible is essential to ensure a set of high-quality inputs, ultimately leading to a good decision. The six input parameters are as follows:

1. **Leadership commitment to decision quality and pace**

   In order to make decisions of the highest quality and most efficient pace, leaders must prioritize both decision quality and decision speed. To this end, effective instruments should be implemented, as shown by Kathleen M. Eisenhardt's study in the high-velocity microcomputer industry. Organizations must establish clear targets for quality and pace using a decision-making protocol (Eisenhardt, 1989). For example, the leadership team should adopt a process that combines human insight, data, analytics, machine learning, and AI to establish logical parameters (Davenport & Harris, 2007). This approach necessitates a democratized decision-making process that departs from historical precedent. In making decisions, leaders should rely on input from key advisors and their professional instincts honed from years of experience (Prahalad & Hamel, 1994).

2. **Processes and tools**

   Next, leaders should focus on decision processes and tools. They need to make sure their decision processes are a good fit for the decisions they often make. In simple terms, leaders should create and use key decision documents and keep them up to date (Nutt, 2008).

   For instance, a company specializing in manufacturing might face frequent decisions related to supply chain management, production scheduling, and quality control. By developing decision-making processes and tools tailored to these specific types of decisions, the company can improve both the speed and quality of its decision-making. This might involve creating a centralized database for suppliers, designing a real-time production monitoring system, or implementing a robust quality control process. By refining and adapting these processes over time, the company can respond more effectively to changes in its operating environment and maintain a competitive edge.

3. **Roles, responsibility, and accountability**

   Give people the power to make decisions based on their knowledge, skills, and experience, not just their job titles (Raelin & Cataldo, 2011). This means letting experts lead the way in their areas of expertise. For example, think about a company that needs to make a big decision about a technical problem. In this situation, a senior engineer might know more about the issue than the vice president. Even though the vice president is in charge, the engineer's insights are more important for making the best decision in this case. This matters because when people feel responsible but also nervous, their thinking might not be as clear as it needs to be (Kahneman, 2011). By letting the most informed, experienced, or knowledgeable people make certain decisions, companies can take the necessary steps that lead to good decisions.

4. **Stakeholder involvement**

   Involve stakeholders in the decision-making process from the start and keep them involved throughout. When making complex decisions, it is important to remember that the choices made by one group can affect other groups, both inside and outside the organization (Freeman, 2010). To ensure everyone gets what they need, bring stakeholders into the process and listen to their input (Harrison & Wicks, 2013). This way, the decisions made will be more inclusive, representative of the needs of everyone involved, and successful.

5. **Data-backed decision-making**

   The quality of decisions relies on the quality of data and technology. To make informed choices, gather information from within and outside the organization to comprehensively understand the situation. This is often a complex decision that involves multiple factors that are beyond human processing abilities. As a result, using analytics, machine learning, and artificial intelligence, along with significant processing power and extensive data, is essential to making well-informed decisions (Provost & Fawcett, 2013).

6. **Mental state of the decision-makers**

   The final component for ensuring decision quality is the mental state of the decision-makers themselves. For non-automated decisions, human involvement is inevitable, and in such cases, the cognitive performance of the group involved in decision-making becomes vital for achieving desired results (Nemeth & Kwan, 1987). Neuroscience and behavioral science research highlight the importance of psychological safety, intrinsic motivation, and group flow in optimizing cognitive function for group decision-making and innovation (Csikszentmihalyi, 1990; Edmondson, 1999).

To enhance all decisions involving human input, it is crucial to educate individuals on metacognition and maintain their optimal mental states throughout the day for quality decision-making (Kahneman, 2011). In simpler terms, this sentence means that to improve decisions that involve people, it is important to teach them about understanding and controlling their thought processes (metacognition). Additionally, ensuring that their mental states are at their best during the day is essential for making high-quality decisions. For instance, individuals should make crucial decisions when they are in the best cognitive state, supported by sufficient sleep, a balanced diet, regular exercise, a high-trust work environment with a clear shared purpose, and dedicated time for contemplation, all of which contribute to optimal brain chemistry for making decisions (Kahneman, 2011; Rock, 2008).

Organizations can cultivate a learning and improvement culture by harnessing data, algorithms, and machine learning, enabling individuals and groups to collaborate, experiment, and ultimately drive innovation and change (Davenport & Harris, 2007).

In the present day and moving forward, emerging trends in decision-making also include an increasing focus on ethics and sustainability. This means that decision-makers are more concerned with the long-term impacts of their decisions on people and the planet rather than just short-term gains.

Decision-making in a globalized and interconnected world is also becoming more complex, as decisions (even operational ones) made in one part of the world can have far-reaching impacts on other regions. As the world becomes more interconnected and technology advances, decision-making has become increasingly complex.

In the following chapters, we will explore Decision Intelligence. We will see how new technology changes our choices in a complex world. So come with us as we travel through history and toward the future, where good decisions and human creativity come together to make amazing things happen.

Before we jump into the topic of Decision Intelligence and the new wave of AI-driven decision-making, let's take a quick tour on the history of decision-making; as the saying goes, "If you want to know the future, look at the past."[2] As we learn from the past, we can get ready for the future.

The History of Decision-Making

As Heraclitus supposedly informed us, "Change is the only constant in life." This wise adage reminds us of the necessity to adapt and evolve our thinking continually. As we delve into the fascinating history of decision-making, our understanding of this complex process has transformed over time, shaped by the contributions of influential thinkers, groundbreaking theories, and technological advancements

From the dawn of the Industrial Revolution to the cutting-edge decision-making technologies of today, our understanding of decision-making has evolved dramatically. This journey takes us through the vibrant landscape of history, weaving together the

---

[2]This aphorism has been credited to a number of people, from Albert Einstein to the turtle in *Kung Fu Panda*.

contributions of influential thinkers, groundbreaking theories, and technological advancements that have shaped the decision-making landscape.

During the Industrial Revolution (1760s–1830s), the world witnessed a disruptive shift in decision-making processes. The emergence of corporations and the development of modern management techniques, championed by pioneers like Frederick Taylor and Henri Fayol, required more structured and efficient approaches to decision-making for organizations to thrive. Taylor's scientific management principles and Fayol's administrative theory laid the groundwork for systematic decision-making processes in the industrial era, focusing on increased productivity and improved efficiency.

Visionaries such as Adam Smith and John Stuart Mill also profoundly impacted decision-making during this period. Smith's *The Wealth of Nations* emphasized the importance of specialization and division of labor, while Mill's utilitarianism philosophy advocated for decisions that maximized overall happiness. These ideas contributed significantly to the evolution of decision-making, shaping how businesses operated and making their mark on the economic landscape.

Picture yourself stepping into a factory during the Industrial Revolution, where workers' performance was measured down to the second, and every aspect of their tasks was optimized for maximum efficiency. These principles of time-and-motion studies, which aimed to streamline processes and reduce waste, have continued to influence modern organizations even into the 21st century. Surprisingly, however, not a lot has changed. Today's businesses still seek ways to enhance productivity and performance with the same mindset of the past, often misusing data-driven approaches, sophisticated technology, and advanced analytics to underline their decisions.

As we reflect on this era, we see that the Industrial Revolution transformed how goods were produced and revolutionized the decision-making processes within organizations. The focus on efficiency, productivity, and specialization laid the foundation for modern management practices, which continue to evolve in response to the ever-changing business landscape. Nevertheless, the lessons learned from this period remain relevant, serving as a reminder of the importance of adaptability, innovation, and strategic decision-making in pursuing success.

When the curtain rose on the 20th century, events such as the World Wars took center stage, propelling the development of game theory and systems thinking. These innovative approaches aimed to model complex decision-making situations involving multiple participants and interdependent outcomes. Meanwhile, the rise of behavioral economics, championed by Herbert Simon, Daniel Kahneman, and Amos Tversky, shed light on the deviations from rational decision-making that define human behavior.

The early 20th century witnessed the birth of decision-making theories in fields such as economics and psychology. The likes of John von Neumann, Oskar Morgenstern, Leon Festinger, and Daniel Kahneman explored the intricate cognitive processes that underlie decision-making. Their pioneering research challenged the notion of humans as perfectly rational decision-makers, unveiling the subtle interplay of emotions and biases that color our choices.

As the mid-20th century unfolded, decision science emerged as a formal interdisciplinary field, uniting researchers from diverse backgrounds to develop innovative models and tools to navigate the labyrinth of choices. Mathematical models and statistical methods, such as decision analysis and decision theory, captured the complex trade-offs and uncertainties in decision-making, providing tangible tools for solving real-life problems.

The thrilling decades of the 1970s and 1980s saw researchers dive into the uncharted waters of heuristics, biases research, and prospect theory (Kahneman & Tversky, 1979). These new approaches added depth and complexity to our understanding of human choices (e.g. taking into account the expected risk of potential outcomes), further challenging traditional rational decision-making models.

As the 1990s and 2000s rolled in, significant advancements in behavioral decision research, cognitive psychology, and neuroscience continued to reshape our understanding of decision-making. The emergence of computational methods, big data, and machine learning algorithms gave decision-makers powerful tools for analyzing complex information and making informed choices.

Our understanding of decision-making has evolved through various stages, driven by the works of influential thinkers, the development of new theories, and the integration of technology. The result is a fascinating and multifaceted portrait of human decision-making that continues to evolve as we push the boundaries of knowledge and technology. This captivating narrative invites us to explore the myriad factors that shape our choices and inspires us to embrace the complex beauty of human decision-making.

As we will see in this book, especially over the course of the last 20 years, the convergence of artificial intelligence (AI), machine learning, and big data analytics provides powerful tools for decision-makers, enabling more precise and informed choices in various sectors, such as healthcare, finance, and environmental management.

As decision-making research progresses, integrating technology and human insight offers promising opportunities for navigating an increasingly complex world. For instance, AI-powered decision support systems can aid physicians in diagnosing diseases, suggesting treatment plans, and predicting patient outcomes. In finance, robo-advisors and algorithmic trading systems can help investors make better-informed decisions, balancing risk and reward based on individual preferences and market conditions. In environmental management, AI-driven models can forecast and mitigate the effects of climate change, guiding policymakers in crafting effective strategies for a more sustainable future.

The Impact of Technology on Business Decision-Making in the 21st Century

In 1997, the world's greatest chess player, Gary Kasparov, faced off against IBM's Deep Blue computer in a historic match. Kasparov, who had won a match the year before, eventually lost that game. While studying the patterns of human and machine, he recognized the potential of combining human intuition and creativity with computer calculations and analysis. He went on to organize a series of advanced chess tournaments, in which human players were allowed to consult with computers during the game. Kasparov's efforts to combine human and machine intelligence were groundbreaking. They ultimately helped to expand the possibilities of chess and enhance the understanding of the relationship between human and machine intelligence.

In general, the impact of technology on business decision-making in the 21st century has been significant, with algorithms outperforming humans in an increasing number of games and decision-making challenges (Silver et al., 2016). This technological innovation has revolutionized various aspects of business operations, enabling businesses to collect, analyze, and interpret large amounts of data in real time, resulting in improved adaptation and increased awareness. The study by Yan Li, Zijun Li, and Li Zhang (2017) on credit scoring, for example, showed that machine learning algorithms can provide more accurate and efficient credit scoring than conventional models. This has significant implications for the financial industry, where credit scoring is a critical aspect of risk management and lending decisions. Several other studies have shown the potential for machine learning algorithms to outperform conventional credit scoring models, like Khandani, Kim, and Lo (2010) found that machine learning algorithms could predict defaults more accurately than traditional models based on credit scores and other financial information.

As we will see in later parts of this book, big data and artificial intelligence are increasingly being used to support, augment, and replace human decision-making in a variety of domains. While there are significant benefits to using these technologies, there are also important challenges to be addressed, such as interpretability and fairness.

More reliance on technology may lead to a lack of critical thinking, reduced empathy, and an erosion of human agency. The potential for biases in AI algorithms stemming from the data and assumptions used to train these systems can lead to unfair or discriminatory[3] outcomes.

Cynthia Rudin's study in 2019, along with other researchers, has emphasized the need for interpretability in machine learning algorithms. Doshi-Velez and Kim proposed in 2017 a taxonomy for interpretability that distinguishes between different types of explanations, such as feature relevance, decision rules,

---

[3]There are many examples and studies regarding potential biases and the challenge of controlling them in business application as rating systems or recruiting (see e.g. "Amazon scraps secret AI recruiting tool that showed bias against women" (Dastin, 2018).

and counterfactuals. Other researchers have proposed techniques for visualizing and explaining the inner workings of complex machine learning models, most commonly known as *Explainable AI*. And finally, data privacy and security topics are of course a big discussion point while looking at the advantages of AI and Big Data.

Fast forward to today, when new AI capabilities are being developed and released at an unbelievable pace and we have access to unprecedented amounts of data. While some organizations have quickly translated this into a competitive advantage, arguably only very few individuals and organizations truly know how to leverage the promise of these developments to make better, higher-quality decisions. Ongoing research and development in these areas will be crucial to realizing the full potential of Big Data and artificial intelligence in decision-making and must not overlook the downsides and governance issues.

For many tech companies, those data- and machine-supported decision-making processes and automation are completely normal. Automated forecasts and recommendation engines especially in customer-facing applications are market standard and also raise customer expectations for high-quality decisions that are made quickly and regularly. Just think of the recommendation engines in TikTok, Spotify, and Netflix or commonly used features like autocorrect, translations, autocomplete, and many more. These developments are now also making their way into all other business areas.

Organizations and decision-makers must remain vigilant in assessing the impact of technology on the decision-making process, ensuring that human values and interests are not overshadowed by algorithmic efficiency. By blending the best of human intuition and empathy with the computational power of AI, we can navigate the challenges of an increasingly complex world, making better decisions for individuals, communities, and the planet.

The future of decision-making will likely involve a symbiotic relationship between human insight and advanced technologies, such as AI and machine learning. By harnessing the strengths of both, we can tackle complex problems, make more informed choices, and drive meaningful progress. As researchers continue to explore the fascinating world of decision-making, new theories and methodologies will undoubtedly emerge, further enriching our understanding of human behavior and guiding us through life's ever-evolving decision-making landscape.

Regaining the Human Aspects

As impressive as those developments and possibilities are, the question of which part of decision-making belongs to the human is getting more and more attention. The book *Sensemaking: The Power of the Humanities in the Age of the Algorithm* by Christian Madsbjerg underscores the importance of human intuition, empathy, and creativity in decision-making, especially in navigating complex business challenges. The author argues that in a world that is increasingly data-driven, organizations tend to rely heavily on quantitative analysis and technological tools and, in turn, to disregard the essential role of human insight in understanding the needs and desires of customers, employees, and other stakeholders (Madsbjerg, 2017). The book provides several examples of successful companies that have embraced a more human-centered approach to decision-making, such as IBM, Lego, and Ford. For instance, IBM used design thinking to develop a new approach to customer service that involved empathy and understanding the customer's perspective, leading to more effective and personalized solutions.

Example

The LEGO Group was facing a crisis in the early 2000s, as the company's profits were declining and its products were losing relevance. Instead of relying solely on market research and consumer feedback, the company's leaders decided to engage in sensemaking, which involved spending time with children and observing how they played with LEGO bricks. Through this process, the company realized that children were not just interested in building pre-designed sets, but also in using their imaginations to create their own designs. This led to a shift in the company's product development strategy, with a renewed focus on encouraging creativity and imagination in children. This approach helped LEGO to regain its competitive edge and become one of the world's most successful toy companies.

(Madsbjerg & Rasmussen, 2014)

Furthermore, Madsbjerg emphasizes the significance of empathy, curiosity, and cross-disciplinary thinking in decision-making, because these characteristics help leaders to question their assumptions, challenge their biases, and consider multiple perspectives before making a decision. He also encourages leaders and innovators to embrace ambiguity and uncertainty, because they can lead to new opportunities for growth and development. In the context of decision-making, Madsbjerg highlights the importance of integrating human insights with data-driven analysis to arrive at informed and effective decisions. By valuing human intuition, empathy, and creativity, organizations can make better decisions that are aligned with the needs and expectations of stakeholders, leading to improved outcomes and long-term success.

In this book we advocate both aspects – the incredible power and potential of the technological developments that are ready to be democratized and used in applications throughout companies, and the human aspect around intuition, strategic thinking, contextual/domain expertise, and human biases – and we examine why traditional decision-making is broken.

CHAPTER

2

Why Traditional Decision-Making Is Broken

"The future belongs to those who can navigate the complexities and uncertainties of our rapidly changing world with confidence and creativity."

– Richard Branson

In recent years, there has been huge hype around methods that have long been used in very innovative and highly dynamic challenges, such as in product innovation. Iterative planning tools and cycles, agile working (see also Chapters 7 and 8), design thinking, and simulations are increasingly finding resonance even in more traditional industries and sectors. The explanation is that environmental complexity and the speed of change have increased dramatically, posing extreme challenges for companies in almost all areas. And the global influences of pandemics, supply chain difficulties, political instabilities, and rapidly changing user behavior have now reached even the most remote corners of corporate reality. Moreover, if we look at possible success factors for dealing with the new challenges, one thing can be said: traditional approaches and decision-making in this environment are not promising. Why is that?

The New (Corporate) Normal: An Increasingly Dynamic and Complex Reality with Uncertainties

Let's take a closer look at the two major influences. The first one is **speed of change.** Many organizations have learned and developed structures, patterns, strategies, planning cycles, and decision-making processes in a time when customer demands were a lot more stable, supply chains were not as uncertain as they are now, and trends and changes in markets and technologies were not as extremely dynamic. There are numerous examples demonstrating the speed of change. Here are two:

1. *New products, technologies, and services change the market and the user behavior at a dramatically increased speed.*

   There are many studies on the increasingly accelerated user growth of market-changing products and technologies (and when we reflect on it we don't need any studies, because we see and feel it in our day-to-day life). The path to 100 million monthly users from the time of market entry took more than five years for Twitter in 2006 (one of the fastest-growing services at the time), about three and a half years for WhatsApp, and two and a half years for Instagram. By contrast, TikTok took only about nine months in 2017, and ChatGPT reached 100 million users in less than two months (!) when it entered the market in 2023 (see Figure 2.1). This means that companies need to be much more flexible and adapt faster to new products, services, and technologies. And this no longer

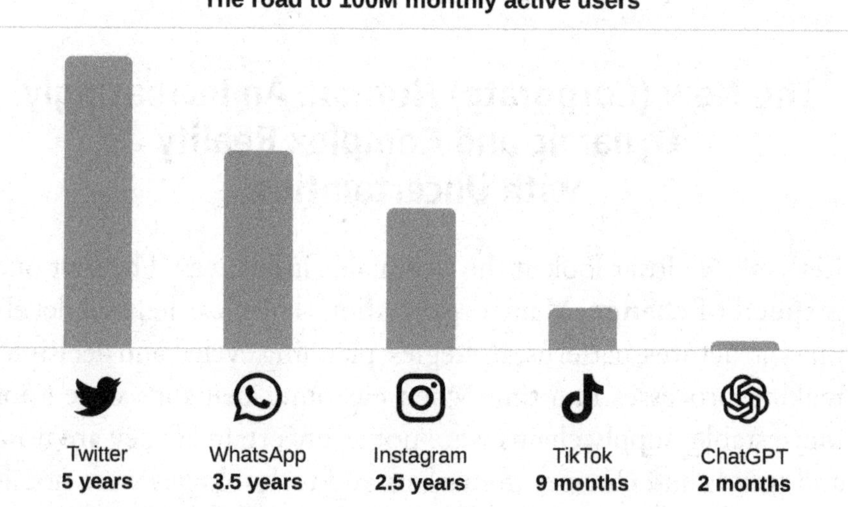

FIGURE 2.1 The road to 100 million monthly active users.

applies only to product development and innovation teams, but now affects large parts of the company.

2. *Technology is a key component for social change.*

We can still remember it all too well: in the early days of the digitization wave, in almost every company presentation, photos from the 2005 and 2013 papal elections taken at St. Peter's Square served as a comparison for how quickly technology has advanced in just a few years. In 2005, there were hardly any cell phones to be seen, while in 2013, practically everyone had a tablet or cell phone in their hand to take a photo or video. Chronologically, this is just seven years apart, but in terms of technological development, this photo symbolizes a leap of the century.

When we discussed including this "old" example here in the book, we wondered if it would be possible to develop this series further. And indeed, a photo went viral globally with the hashtag #selfiegeneration during the 2016 US presidential election (see e.g. Graham, 2016). The photo captured a campaign event featuring Hillary Clinton in a packed room, where almost all attendees were taking selfies of themselves "in the moment," with their backs facing the candidate. Sociologically speaking, there was an evident shift on social media toward showcasing "me in the moment," indicating one's presence at a particular event or location.

However, this phenomenon is not solely the result of societal trends interacting with technology; other external factors may also be at play. The 2020 COVID pandemic moved many gatherings, meetings, and even events completely online. In addition, the 2020 election campaign was predominantly conducted digitally due to lockdown. This example clearly demonstrates how technology, user behavior, and social aspects have undergone dramatic changes in just a few years. And of course, this can be observed in other areas as well, including shopping, mobility, and information search and consumption.

Now, the intriguing question is: Who could have predicted the next photo five years in advance? This is difficult to impossible, which is exactly why it is so important to remain adaptable to changing circumstances. Think about it for yourself from today's perspective: What will the next election or other major event look like in three to five years? Will it take place in a complete virtual reality like the metaverse, will it mean we speak to avatars, will it involve new AI technologies? It's hard to imagine, isn't it?

Key Challenge: Increasing Environmental Complexity

Complex systems are characterized by numerous elements and properties that interact in dynamic ways. These elements are often unstable and interconnected, making it difficult to identify causality and dependencies. As a result, it is not always possible to recognize all dependencies or predict future causalities. Furthermore, the dynamic interactions of these elements result in emergence, which is behavior that cannot be directly derived from individual elements' characteristics.

A prime example of a complex system is a forest ecosystem, comprising various species and interactions among plants, trees, soil, insects, and birds. The behavior of these species is often unpredictable due to mutual interdependencies. Another example is social systems such as businesses or political organizations, where individuals, stakeholders, and behaviors interact in ways that affect outcomes unpredictably.

For the comparison between complicated and complex, let us take a look at an example of a *complicated* system: the construction of an airplane. It is indeed not *easy* to build, but it can be described in detail and follows clear physical laws and mechanisms. In other words, it can be built repeatedly according to a construction plan. Or to put it in a more generalized way, it is quite possible to make explicit derivations in linear, complicated systems, which are arranged with clear hierarchies or structures and can be controlled by fixed rules or laws.

In the digitalized world, however, many systems we look at every day are more *complex*, not *complicated*. To build a completely new social media platform, to develop an AGI (artificial general intelligence) with a chat interface, to navigate a company in all the uncertainties – these are all complex tasks that require creative and iterative solutions. The uncertainties of broken supply chains, the consequences of a virus outbreak or political conflicts also increase system complexity for many areas in companies. Another difficulty for companies and the management is that complex systems and challenges often emerge in the same organization alongside existing complicated ones. For example, for a car manufacturer building a car is a complicated problem, while building a digital mobility platform is a complex challenge.

In addition to the cultural challenges (the recent shift to more iterative, agile approaches with a high degree of self-organization) that are needed to effectively address these complexities, management teams and companies are facing a massive problem: traditional, linear considerations and predictions also fail as a basis for decision-making at this point.

If there is a straightforward way to get started with the topic and one that is easy to implement practically, then we would always recommend the Cynefin framework (see Figure 2.2), a very valuable and widely used model to classify in which system state the respective challenge is and – more importantly – to identify reasonable solution strategies for the various system types. Developed by management expert Dave Snowden, it has quickly gained a reputation in the business world and is used by many leading companies worldwide. It is an excellent tool to classify the different challenges you want to tackle and to evaluate the approaches

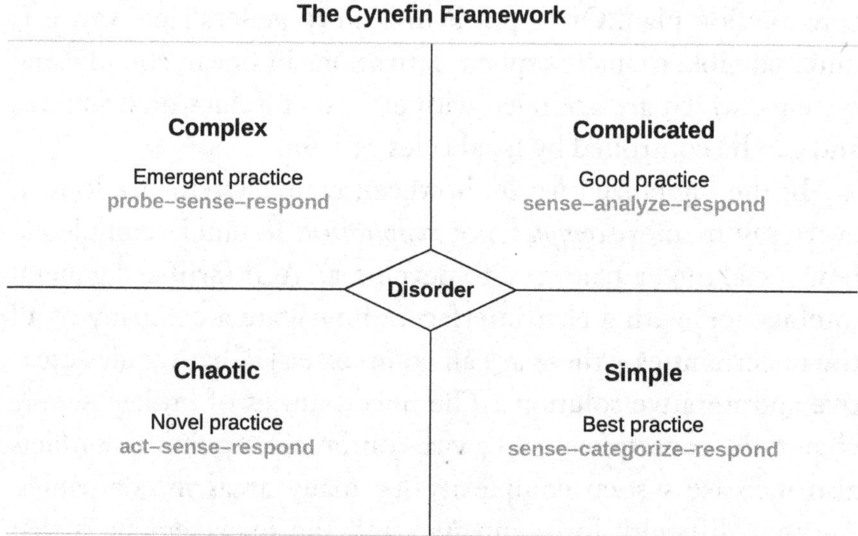

FIGURE 2.2 The Cynefin framework.

to solve them.[1] "The framework sorts the issues facing leaders into five contexts defined by the nature of the relationship between cause and effect. . . . and . . . require[s] leaders to diagnose situations and to act in contextually appropriate ways" (Snowden & Boone, 2007).

According to Snowden, there are four states of systems and corresponding solution strategies (and a fifth state, which is "disorder," when it is unclear which of the four contexts is predominant).

1. **Simple**. Problems that are simple have clear cause-and-effect relationships and there are proven methods to solve them. In this area, it is best to use known practices and apply proven solutions. This is about applying "best practices" and standards to achieve effective solutions.

[1] And very often we use it to discover why initiatives in companies are not very successful or to support a digital/data transformation coaching with executives as most of the strategies of traditional companies are completely based on "best practices" (which makes no sense at all, as we see here).

A successful solution strategy for a SIMPLE challenge can be described as "sense-categorize-respond."

2. **Complicated**. Complicated problems also have cause-and-effect relationships, but there is not just one obvious solution. In this area, it is important to use expert knowledge and specialized techniques and consider different options to find the best solution. Accurate, expert guidance and "good practices" are sound guides here, even if it takes a fair amount of analysis.

   The right solution strategy for a COMPLICATED challenge is "sense-analyze-respond."

3. **Complex**. Complex problems, as described above, have many interrelated factors and interactions that are not always predictable. This is about testing ideas and learning from mistakes because there is no simple solution; you must find solutions through experimentation and adaptation. Since it makes no sense to copy good or best practices from others, this is also referred to as "emergent practices."

   The best solution strategy for a COMPLEX challenge can be defined as "probe-sense-respond."

4. **Chaotic**. In this area, there are no clear cause-and-effect relationships at all and there is a high level of uncertainty. Decisions must be made quickly in order to regain control of the situation, even if you are not sure if it is the right (or good) decision. The point is to quickly stabilize the situation and establish a foundation for further resolution.

   The best solution strategy for a CHAOTIC challenge is "act-sense-respond."

In the context of this book and the topic of Decision Intelligence, looking at the third category of *complex problems* is crucial. In our experience working with management teams, we very often see attempts to identify a "good practice" or even "best practice" for next steps in the context of a complex challenge. While these are good approaches to solving simple and complicated challenges, they are designed to fail in complex environments. (Have you ever tried to use traditional keys with fingerprint sensors?)

Example

We supported a company developing a new product/service for a new market segment. Although there were no role models or similar products, and the market was very complex and just emerging, the traditionally minded management team kept asking for "best practices." When we introduced the Cynefin framework to the leadership team, it had a "wow" effect and eventually gave the product team the freedom to experiment and iterate.

Moreover, it is a human urge to simplify challenges as a solution strategy. We know this from our daily lives: When complex product comparisons are too exhausting for us, we reduce the considerations to the *price* – that is, to a simple attribute. Or, to put it more theoretically, we try to make many complex problems manageable by simplifying them to a simple system state. If we look at this in the light of the Cynefin framework, it becomes clear that this is not a sustainable solution strategy. We as humanity and as an organization must finally learn to manage complexity!

To summarize, decision-making is broken, because organizations are still managing **speed of change** and **increasing complexity** with the thinking patterns, solution approaches, and tools of the past. Those two major effects lead to many new challenges in nearly every part of the organization. In addition, they are often interconnected and accelerate each other. As an example, just take a look at how small changes in demand with uncertainties in supply can have a whiplash-like effect in many supply chains today.[2] This leads to great uncertainty and suboptimal, inefficient decisions (and, in the end, unhappy customers).

Why Data Analytics and Business Intelligence Can't Keep up with the New Reality

Over the past few years, it seems like almost every company we are familiar with has undertaken multiple data projects, integrated data lakes and data warehouses, and initiated business intelligence (BI) initiatives. To keep up with the types of challenges discussed above, they have leveraged the use of data analytics and BI to react and adapt faster. In addition, a few implemented process mining and robotic process automation (RPA) to optimize and automate processes. But given our context, this is only the foundation for the next evolution: prescriptive analytics and Decision Intelligence (see Figure 2.3). This will enable organizations around the globe to take a leap toward the ultimate goal here: derive actionable insights.

Data Analytics and Business Intelligence

Key question: What can we learn by analyzing structured data?

The urge to make well-informed and therefore better decisions led to the need for reliable, cross-company, and well-structured data. And the good news is that analytics is still the

[2] This is why this is called *bullwhip effect* in economic literature.

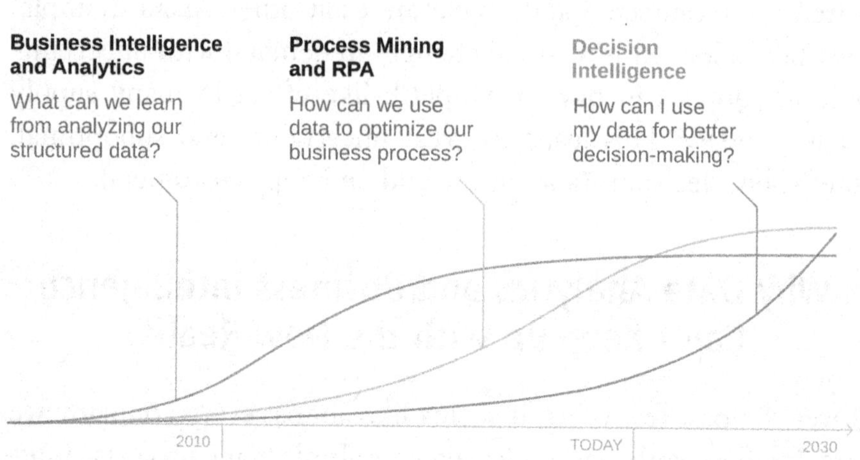

FIGURE 2.3 Decision Intelligence, the business trend of the future.

first step to a data-supported decision. Monitoring data, connecting different streams in the company, and mapping it to business challenges and in the goal-setting process is a crucial starting point for many other initiatives. However, these efforts only address the question of *what we can learn by analyzing structured data*, which applies to both historical and near-real-time data. But this form of analysis is still like a view in the rear-view mirror.

In addition, it's safe to say that the amount of data being generated and collected is growing exponentially, thanks to the rise of digital technologies and the proliferation of connected devices. The sheer volume of information that is available can be complex in and of itself, with multiple variables and factors that need to be considered in order to make accurate predictions or decisions.

Let's take a quick look at the figures to grasp the level of complexity we're talking about. According to a forecast from a Statista study, the amount of data generated globally is expected to reach 181 zettabytes (ZB) by 2025 (Statista, 2021). This abstrusely high number is neither tangible nor can the human brain even begin to process this amount of information.[3]

No wonder data present both opportunities and challenges for businesses. On the one hand, they can be used to gain insights; on the other hand, managing and processing such a large amount of data is extremely complex and time-consuming. To be able to maintain an overview and learn from their own corporate data, organizations must embrace complexity instead of trying to reduce it at all costs.

Process Mining and RPA

Key question: What can we learn by analyzing structured data?

When it comes to the optimization of processes, the next level of this data analysis evolution was the rise of *process mining*. Let's take a typical repetitive process such as the procurement process, also called *purchase to pay*. Since the processes are now mostly digitized and it is moreover possible to collect metadata from various enterprise resource planning (ERP) and procurement tools (for example, how much time the procurement employee spends processing the document or how often it is forwarded), it is possible to visualize this process and find bottlenecks and optimization potential. With this approach and a given tool it is possible to find potential savings and efficiencies in processes across different departments in organizations.

---

[3]The "zettabyte era" has a great impact on business processes and decisions too. Although the amount of data that each business has to collect and process obviously varies greatly depending on its size and type, there seems to be a shared attribute that is further increasing the level of complexity for business decisions: the form of data available in companies: 95% of businesses cite the need to manage unstructured data as a problem for their business (Kulkarni, 2019).

The next logical step we can think of is a higher level of automation within a given process as described by *robotic process automation*. This involves identifying processes or process steps where bots can be used to fully automate an optimized process, potentially replacing manual work, or reducing the workload to save even more money. This approach holds tremendous potential to increase efficiency in companies, as reflected by the success of companies and tools in the process mining and RPA industry.

Decision Intelligence and Prescriptive Analytics

Key question: How can I use my data for better decision-making?

Let's return to the more complex and dynamic challenges. Today, we require a greater degree of intelligence than simply looking for efficiencies in repetitive processes, where the ultimate question becomes: *How can I use my data for better decision-making?*

This is the point where analytics, BI, and process mining falls short, and precisely where Decision Intelligence comes into play. As we already have concluded, we need a distinct approach to address complex and dynamic problems – one that is nonlinear and iterative. Machine learning models and more sophisticated optimization algorithms are essential in this scenario, requiring a significantly different (and more complex) technological infrastructure than what is required for analytics or process mining.

For this reason, Decision Intelligence is one of the most crucial topics for companies in the years to come. According to the leading analyst research firms, nearly every company will introduce DI over the next years (see e.g. Rollings, 2021) and it will cover a $22.7 billion market in 2027 (see e.g. Markets&Markets, 2023). This area is often also referred to as *prescriptive analytics* because (compared to predictive analytics) it also provides actionable recommendations and decision options.

However, how can organizations integrate this approach to transform *data-centric* into *decision-centric* strategies? And how can we, as humans, oversee the process from data to decisions? Is it still needed to incorporate human intuition as part of the solution?

As such, in the next section, we will explore the role of human intuition in the modern decision-making process, before diving deeper into the intricacies of Decision Intelligence itself.

The Illusion of Human Control: Will We Ever Be Able to Make the Best Possible Choice?

As we have observed, the sheer volume and complexity of data can be challenging for the human brain to process. However, it turns out that a skill once deemed negative or unprofessional (at least in the organizational context) can be a valuable guide in tackling complex challenges: **intuition.** And by that we don't mean the common meaning of "gut feeling," but rather a professionally trained and used intuition that helps us beyond a rational understanding.

According to Kruse, a complexity researcher and cognitive psychologist who has synthesized insights from brain research and theories on dynamic systems, this kind of intuition is a potent force. This means that humans are able to manage complexity in their brains in a fascinating way by forming patterns and being reliable at detecting patterns within complex systems. The bad news is that developing these skills requires a lot of training. Or as Kruse puts it, almost philosophically, "It is only when you are acting intuitively you should have had a very long learning history on the verge of being overwhelmed" (Kruse, 2008, 2:30).

Consequently, it is necessary to train our brains for effectively harnessing our intuition. Nevertheless, the rapid changes in the environment pose a great challenge, as aptly summarized by Kruse:

> With intuition, we now have . . . a gigantic solution for dealing with complexity – we just have a huge problem: If the world has changed in between, then my intuitions that have formed yesterday still feel just as safe today as they did before – just unfortunately completely off. Because the context in which I trained the intuitions is no longer the context in which I want to use them today.
>
> (Kruse, 2008, 2:46)

In other words: our trained pattern-recognition skills play a big trick on us when it comes to changing requirements. This phenomenon is actually something we encounter extremely often in organizations, particularly among individuals in managerial positions or those responsible for making day-to-day operational decisions.

However, this finding also means that we can only get out of this trap if we recognize and form new patterns as a strategy for success through constant reflection, review, and ultimately also trial-and-error and experimentation. If this is a very difficult (and as Prof. Kruse noted, lengthy) process for humans, this is where machine learning models come into play. In the repeated practice and recognition of patterns, even in large and complex data sets, lies the chance to react and adapt much faster; the new generations of neural networks in particular (such as Transformer models and Large Language models) have a clear advantage here. By the way, the T in GPT stands for Transformer, which refers to the neural network architecture used in the *Generative Pre-trained Transformer* models. Thus, even in complex and always dynamically changing systems, machine-learning-based predictions and recommendations can be made that are ahead of human intuition or become strong in combination therewith. As strong as AI is in this area, we will see later in the book that humans add two important ingredients to the soup besides intuition: *strategy* and *context*.

To sum it up, it was important for us to explain why traditional decision-making is broken. The tools and approaches around data and visualization need a makeover (and yes, this also counts for Excel!).[4] The result is bad and slow decision-making. And it is a *real* pain. McKinsey extrapolated its survey results to the top US companies in terms of revenue:

> Ineffective decision-making has significant implications for company productivity. On average, respondents spend just 37% of their time making decisions and, even worse, more than half of this time was thought to be spent ineffectively. For managers at an average Fortune 500 company, this could translate to more than 530,000 days of lost working time and roughly $250 million of wasted labor costs per year.
>
> (Aminov et al., 2019)

The good news is that there are new and better approaches to tackle the challenges that we are all facing in a more complex and dynamic world.

[4] No kidding, Excel is still the most common tool we see in organizations trying to manage specific operations in addition to other tools to manage complexity and dynamics.

CHAPTER

3

Decision Intelligence: Making Relevant Information Visible and Actionable

"If you don't know where you want to go, then it doesn't matter which path you take."

– Lewis Carroll, *Alice in Wonderland*

The breakthrough of Decision Intelligence represents a paradigm shift in strategic business processes, addressing a critical question: How can we transition from "I feel" to "I know"? This shift is particularly relevant in a world that has become so dynamic and complex that both our brain capacity and the traditional solution strategies reach their limits. To fully grasp and implement Decision Intelligence as a young discipline within your organization, it is essential to understand the two dimensions that it encompasses: the domain and context-specific dimension ("Decision") and the technological dimension ("Intelligence").

The domain and context-specific dimension pertains to the given problem and potential outcomes. It recognizes that each decision-making scenario is unique, requiring tailored approaches to understand the complexities and interdependencies involved. On the other hand, the technological dimension focuses on leveraging advanced tools, such as artificial intelligence and machine learning, to augment human decision-making capabilities. These technologies enable organizations to analyze vast amounts of data, uncover hidden patterns, and make informed decisions in a previously impossible way. By bringing together these two dimensions, Decision Intelligence empowers organizations to confidently navigate the intricate landscape of modern business challenges, harnessing the power of data-driven insights and human intuition to make good decisions.

Overall, Decision Intelligence enables you to put decisions at the forefront of your business strategy to remain competitive, meet your customer demands, and foster innovation. Its underlying methodology is a "decision-back approach" (Larson, 2021). It implies that managers start by identifying critical company decisions and work their way back to the data, skills, and means that are needed to make the best possible decision in order to achieve a certain goal. "DI shifts our focus beyond science and systems (including AI) that 'answer questions,' 'provide insights,' or 'make predictions' to those that help us make decisions that guide actions, which lead to outcomes," argues Lorien Pratt. In fact, the computer scientist was one of the first to define the term "Decision Intelligence" and finally bring it to a broader attention in her book *Link: How Decision Intelligence Connects Data, Actions, and Outcomes* (Pratt, 2019).

Secondly, when it comes to outcome-oriented decisions a manager has to make, it is important to understand a problem in all its complexity. That means you must take into account the influence of all the individual and multidimensional factors that make your company decisions so complex, even for recurring operational decisions. That's why Decision Intelligence leverages advanced technologies such as data science and AI/machine learning that can identify patterns, manage complexity, and provide actionable recommendations.

> With Decision Intelligence, companies and teams are able to shift from a **data-centric** approach toward a **decision-centric** approach.

In this chapter, we provide a brief introduction to the concept of Decision Intelligence, the general approach of AI supporting decisions and actions, and the three levels of autonomy and automation in DI.

How to Shift Your Decision-Making Perspective

Take a Decision-First Approach

According to Lorien Pratt (2019), the core principle underlying any decision is this: "If I make this decision, which leads to this action, in these circumstances, today, what will be the outcome tomorrow?" That is, decisions that ultimately lead to *actions*, not to *conclusions*. This differentiation is especially relevant in the context of understanding and optimizing business decisions, since they are the thriving force to build and maintain a profitable company (or optimizing other company targets, such as reducing CO_2 emissions). Any decision that is taken in a company – no matter how small or large the organization is – will lead to specific tasks and measures to be carried out in order to reach a specific business-relevant goal.

Interestingly, this insight of causal triggers and interconnected decisions in organizations is also applied in other areas, such as OKRs (objectives and key results, the iterative planning framework that has been so popular for several years). In our eyes, it completely makes sense, because the idea of triggers to drive the needle of target business KPIs, goals and key results (KRs), and iterative planning cycles is very similar to the input-output view and the iterative retraining of machine learning models. It's like playing with dominoes! Just as you set up dominoes to create a chain reaction, understanding the cause-and-effect relationships in organizations, like those in the popular OKR framework, is similar to how machine learning models learn and adapt. It's all about finding the right pieces and arranging them to make things work smoothly.

That being said, it's the decision (or rather the question that defines a decision) that ties business objectives to operations, not your generated data set or your strategic compass (Decosmo, 2018).

This methodology is often referred as a decision-first approach (as mentioned before, other sources and experts use the term "decision-back approach"). It implies that managers start with identifying critical company decisions and work their way forward to the skills and means that are needed to make the best possible decision in order to achieve a certain goal. In this way, Decision Intelligence enables you to put decisions at the forefront of your business strategy to remain competitive, meet your customer demands, and foster innovation.

Now, you might perceive it as a truism to tie your data analysis insights to actual outcome-oriented decisions. However, this is exactly where companies struggle. While most of them have finally recognized the importance of generating and analyzing their data and spend billions on analytics capabilities and tools, they waste 60% of these investments because they don't link their data to their aspired business goals (Larson, 2021). As a result, critical data-generated insights and recommendations rarely make it to the "decision table" (Larson, 2021) – to be precise, only 22% of the time.

While it's difficult, of course, to measure an exact numerical value, this example shows that many companies and their leaders are operating only in a *data-centric* environment – some are even just getting there (and by the way, this is exactly what we see in our daily work). As a result, most teams are solely focused on constructing a holistic depicting of the organization (what we later refer to as a "digital twin") at extremely high costs, collecting data, and making it accessible. However, it would make much more sense to begin with asking the pertinent business questions (*decisions*) and then reverse-engineer the necessary datapoints and actions and depict not the whole organization but the given problem/decision. Imagine trying to solve a jigsaw puzzle. Instead of dumping all the pieces on the table and trying to assemble the entire picture at once, you first decide which part of the picture you want to focus on, like a specific character or object. Then you gather only the pieces related to that section and assemble them, saving time and effort while addressing the crucial part of the puzzle.

From Data to Knowledge

Honestly speaking, what we have observed over the last couple of years is that numerous companies take pride in proclaiming their ability to extract massive amounts of valuable data and uncover hidden treasures of information. On this basis, they generate reports that reveal lots of facts and figures, but rarely suggest serious and easily comprehensible decisions or recommendations. If you've ever seen an analytics report on the performance of a website that hosts millions of visitors and myriad of content, for example, you will know just how challenging it is to make sense of it, let alone derive a reliable decision for future marketing activities. That is because in most cases the people who actually need to rely on these data sets won't know what they are looking for.

Decision Intelligence shifts the order in which we use data to inform our actions. Instead of mining the data first, which forces us to search for information that could eventually be relevant for our goals, we decide on what we need to know *first* and then choose input, tools, or even strategies to achieve this knowledge. This approach can help companies save time and resources, because data mining in itself becomes more efficient and effective.

> Knowledge is power – data is just information.
>
> (Baker, 2022)

We will take a deeper look at this topic when we dive into the concept of "digital twin" and "causal models" in Chapter 6.

Leverage AI for Decision-Making

Machine-supported decision-making is the most crucial factor when it comes to understand the power of Decision Intelligence, which is why we devoted a whole chapter to data and technology, where you can take a closer look into the engine room of Decision Intelligence.

For now, we just want you to understand the basic principle of how an artificial intelligence fits a modern decision-making process. Thanks to the use of AI systems, advanced technologies help to sort, collect, and process large amounts of related data to draw better and less biased conclusions. They analyze and evaluate the information, identify decision needs, and suggest every available solution. Consideration is given not only to raw data, but also to a multidimensional set of data that could include text, images, video, and audio. Recent machine learning approaches, such as the prominent transformer (neural) networks, are also superior for learning from sparse data or for significant changes in causalities and weights. The results could be used to design alternative solutions and courses of action that decision-makers can follow but, of course, do not have to.

Example

A supply chain unit in a large retail company receives weekly advance notifications from over 100 subdepartments and companies for which they handle shipping and packaging. First, the preregistrations are not very reliable, and second, they would need them on a daily basis because they need to book the shift plan accordingly. The solution was to create their own machine learning supported daily (rolling) forecasts based on historical data and certain other influences (promotion days, weather, vacation periods) and thus optimize the shift plan.

So just like us, machine-learning systems learn from experience and information. They are able to find solutions to recurring and to new and unexpected problems as they prepare the entire process from data analysis to decision recommendation (we will go into detail later on how this is achieved technically). Decision-makers can then make the right decisions by examining the predictions and choosing from all proposed alternatives or actionable recommendations.

Considering all these numerous benefits, isn't it surprising that the number of DI users remains relatively low? Currently, only 38% of companies are really utilizing data-driven approaches to drive their business success (Moreno, 2017). We hope that we can encourage you to drive this important topic forward in your team and in your organization.

> The breakthrough of Decision Intelligence elevates decision-making to an entirely new transformational strategy by future-proofing traditional business intelligence approaches by using AI systems.

The Ultimate Partnership Between Humans and Machines

It is crucial for managers to understand a problem in all its complexity when aiming at outcome-oriented decisions. That means you must take into account the influence of all the individual and multidimensional factors that contribute to the complexity and multifaceted nature of your company's decisions. The driving force behind Decision Intelligence is its ability to correlate multiple factors and identify patterns that can reveal opportunities that may otherwise go unnoticed. This is especially crucial because some managers may rely on personal experience or gut feelings when making choices – a pattern most of us have experienced firsthand.

Now, as we've seen before, organizations are increasingly finding it challenging to surpass the complexity ceiling of an interconnected, data-loaded, competitive business world. For companies and managers seeking to navigate this complexity the most effective strategy is to foster a symbiotic relationship between human and machine intelligence. Together, they can achieve greater success than they would on their own. Or to put it more emphatically, the future belongs to the alliance of human and machine.

However, many managers are still hesitant to leave decision-making to machines, or at least share it with them. But Decision Intelligence is not about science fiction and the disempowerment of mankind by robots. Nor is it some sneaky plan to replace all humans on the job with robots – that is, as long as we don't act like robots ourselves, as Christoph Burkhardt puts it in his book *Don't be a robot* quite nicely: "As humans we have the responsibility to be as human as we can be" (Burkhardt, 2018). So accept this change, and let's do what we can do best: adapt and embrace!

Finding the Balance Between Trust and Control

As car drivers, we face thousands of complex decision-making situations while behind the wheel, where a single wrong move can have fatal consequences within seconds. Isn't it crazy to think that just a few years ago, we wouldn't have even thought about letting machines make life-or-death decisions when we are behind the wheel?

However, over the past few decades, car manufacturers have made significant technological progress in the field of automated driving with the goal of making driving safer and more efficient by handling tasks that are tricky or dangerous for humans to do, like navigating through bumper-to-bumper traffic or driving through a nasty storm. In fact, experts estimate that self-driving cars could even cut down on human error and reduce traffic accidents, at least for specific types of accidents such as pedestrian collisions (Petrović et al., 2020).

As the technology has improved, we have become more comfortable relying on these systems as they have become more reliable and advanced. If you're driving 532 miles from Chicago to Memphis on a long, straight road, things can get pretty dull and your attention can start to drift. That's when many people are happy to let their intelligent driving assistants take the wheel for a while. We are essentially letting the car handle our driving duties and make calls on things like speeding up to pass a slower car or handling unexpected events. And in the future, self-driving cars are even expected to make their own decisions in real-time, predicting what other cars and people are going to do (see Figure 3.1). (Of course, this also raises some big ethical questions that need to be addressed as we keep advancing toward more autonomous driving.)

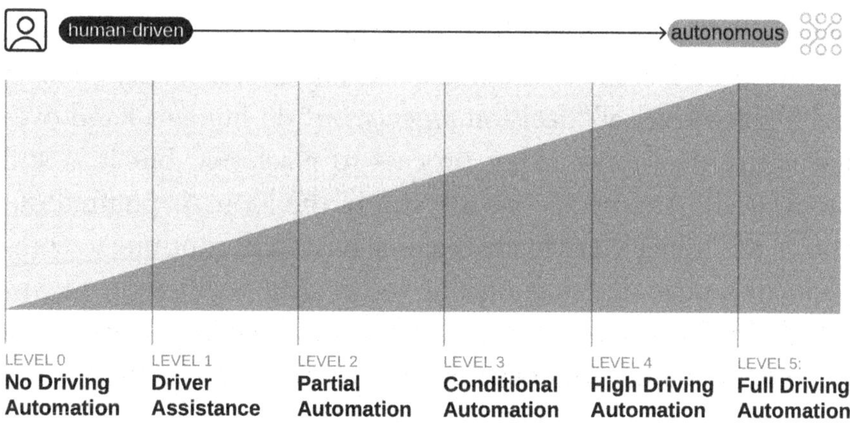

FIGURE 3.1 The six levels of autonomous driving.

As a basis for decision-making about how to navigate the road, a car can collect and process *five gigabytes* of data every minute to help make decisions on the road (ADAC, 2023), based on a variety of sensors and other technologies to perceive their environment. But if the driver takes their hands off the wheel for more than 15 seconds, the system alerts them to pay attention. So we are still responsible for keeping an eye on our car's performance and being ready to take control if needed. The bottom line is that these systems are helpful in empowering our driving behavior, but they can't replace human drivers entirely (at least not yet!).

This example shows why humans and machines need to work together. If we only relied on one or the other, we might not have all the necessary skills and knowledge. Furthermore, we might need to include important details only humans could spot. Plus, if we let machines make all the decisions, we might not be able to hold anyone accountable for what happens, which could lead to a lack of transparency and trust in the decision-making process. It is always important to find a balance between the two.

Three Levels of Decision Intelligence Autonomy

Similar to autonomy levels in autonomous/assisted driving, the spectrum of Decision Intelligence spans several levels. Only at the highest level of "decision *automation*" do humans hand over the entire decision-making process to machines, but it is still monitored by humans – we are still in the loop. As pointed out above, it is much more likely that machines will continue to complement human decision-making rather than taking it over completely in the business context, too (even though, in principle, a wrong judgment here does not run the risk of deciding over life

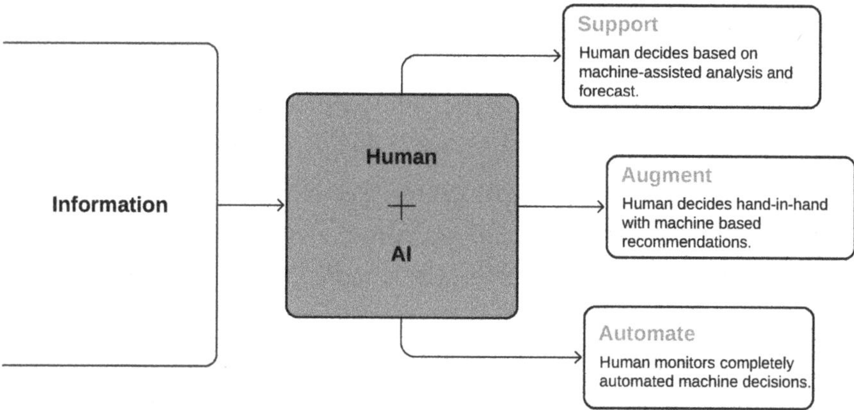

FIGURE 3.2 The three levels of Decision Intelligence augmentation.

and death in most cases). But coming back to the idea of different levels of Decision Intelligence, a very common categorization that is based, among other approaches, on a classification system by Gartner distinguishes between three levels of automation (Rollings, 2021).

Level 1: Decision Support Level 1 comprises tasks that can be solved on the basis of experience or cognitive reasoning, for which support by analyses or data visualizations is usually sufficient. A popular example is the use of clinical decision support systems (CDSS), which enable physicians to access pooled expert knowledge that helps them to make informed diagnoses at an early stage and decide the best course of treatment. Another widespread example is forecasts based on predictions and predictive analytics of a single KPI. As seen in the supply chain example earlier (in the section "Leverage AI for Decision-Making"), we can take decisions just by having an accurate and relevant forecast at hand. We combine it with other information we need for the concrete action and decide manually then.

Example

Imagine you are sitting in a car. The onboard electronics tell you that you can still drive 20 miles with the remaining fuel in the tank. That's a first step forward compared to a classic car, where the fuel needle only indicates that the gasoline is running low (and as we have experienced for ourselves, the needle is sometimes very shaky and inaccurate). The prediction of the system tells you that you now have to make a decision whether to approach the next gas station right now or the one in 17 miles. In the best case, the car's prediction is fed by information about historical consumption, outside temperature, current road conditions, and so on. However, you make the decision yourself, and it is supported by the system.

Level 2: Decision Augmentation Level 2 involves the use of AI systems that are capable of solving more complex problems and already generate recommendations based on predictions from the analyzed data, such as predicting the demand for particular products or services in order to better allocate resources and plan for future demand. The additional support using decision augmentation is therefore the optimal variant for generating recommendations that still need to be explored and evaluated by humans or are part of recurring processes. In other words, humans continue to take the wheel but let themselves be guided in the right direction. The system can give concrete or basic recommendations for action – the decision is taken by a human.

Example

Today, many cars are equipped with navigation software, which will show you not only a range but also the gas stations that you can reach. In a best-case scenario, it can even give you recommendations on which station to use. Ideally, a risk assessment would also be included in the navigation software. This will help you determine how likely it is that you will reach the next gas station, taking into account different factors such as distance, fuel level, terrain, and weather conditions.

Level 3: Decision Automation At this level, machines perform both the decision and the execution autonomously, such as to automatically send targeted emails to customers based on their past purchase history. With decision automation, human involvement in the decision-making process is reduced to the minimum. We can take our hands off the wheel and devote ourselves to other tasks, at least when it comes to our daily business. But of course, just like autonomous cars, AI systems must be regularly monitored and adjusted.

Just think of the Netflix recommendation algorithm as an example. We might have to disappoint you now, but there isn't someone personally selecting movies you might like. The platform's so-called *recommendation engine* is fully automated (as are the recommendation engines of TikTok, Amazon, and Spotify, which are essential components of their services). According to a paper published in 2015 by some Netflix execs, they said that (even back then) the recommendation engine saved Netflix $1 billion per year![1] Nevertheless, humans still control, monitor, and adjust the recommendation engine using meta-parameters, strategies, input factors, and constraints.

---

[1]As this was 2015, we are pretty sure it's worth a lot more now – and this counts also for Amazon, Spotify, TikTok, and the others. Find an overview of various ROIs here: https://www.linkedin.com/pulse/roi-artificial-intelligence-recommendation-systems-petr-popov/, or in the respective paper https://dl.acm.org/doi/10.1145/2843948, both accessed April 7, 2023.

Example

If we now get into an autonomously driving car, then we can simply imagine how the above-mentioned recommendations for action are used by the provider to control the actions of the car completely automatically and to drive to the next gas or charging station.

You see, DI can occur in the wild at various levels of autonomy. Based on the maturity level of the respective team and on the use-case, it makes sense to choose a matching level. Because these are building on top of each other, each level – used for the right business problem – can leverage a huge business value for itself. That's why, before we get into the technical DNA of Decision Intelligence, let's first see where it can actually make a positive impact in organizations, and explore some real-life cases to help us grasp how it works and where it is being applied.

CHAPTER

4

The Business Value of Decision Intelligence

"'The Answer to the Great Question . . . Of Life, the Universe and Everything . . . Is . . . Forty-two,' said Deep Thought, with infinite majesty and calm."

– *Douglas Adams,* The Hitchhiker's Guide to the Galaxy

From Using DI as a Strategy to DecisionOS

Applying AI to decision-making can help your business avoid unnecessary costs due to slow processes and high failure rates. It also enables clear and measurable decision-making, which enhances your company's knowledge management over time. Like top-performing footballers who follow the adage "success must be repeatable," the ability to make optimal decisions consistently and logically is a strong foundation for your company's future success and expansion.

These key benefits make a compelling case for incorporating Decision Intelligence into your organization, ensuring your company stays ahead in a competitive landscape. Think of these benefits as the irresistible aroma of freshly baked cookies. Once your colleagues understand the advantages, they will be eager to learn more and adopt Decision Intelligence in your company.

Making use of complex data sets: AI-driven decision-making processes analyze combinations of previous/historical results and a rich set of information from multiple sources to deliver findings, patterns, results, and pros and cons.

Keeping processes flexible: Technology makes it possible to adjust chosen parameters at any time, depending on situations and requirements. As a result, the company always remains in a position to look at several scenarios, identify a number of alternatives for solving a problem, and decide on the best option. Through retraining, these new parameters can constantly be taken into account through models and the decision-making adjusted accordingly.

Correct and value-free judgment: External factors such as cognitive or behavioral influences as well as human error are more and more eliminated from the entire analysis and evaluation process. The proposed options remain free of bias and error and can show the whole solution space as well as many different possible scenarios.

Making decisions measurable and more transparent: DI provides managers with a system that enables them to track how decisions are made. Key figures and feedback loops make it possible to learn more about processes and how to optimize them. It is also much easier to document and track decisions (which is becoming increasingly important culturally and legally).

Shortening decision-making processes: The analysis process of unorganized and scattered data volumes can be significantly reduced to enable your company to make the right decision in less time. This is especially important for recurring decisions.

Bottom line effect on P&L: In addition to the benefit of leveraging and automating efficiencies, DI has the greatest leverage in realizing unprecedented relevant potential or cost savings through better decision-making. This is the most decisive argument for most C-levels. The challenge is that the results cannot be accurately calculated in advance, but as we show with a couple of examples in this book, the amortization of the implementation costs is usually extremely fast and the levers are huge. (For example, one large parcel delivery company told us that improving the accuracy of forecasts by 5% translates into annual savings of about $20 million to $25 million.)

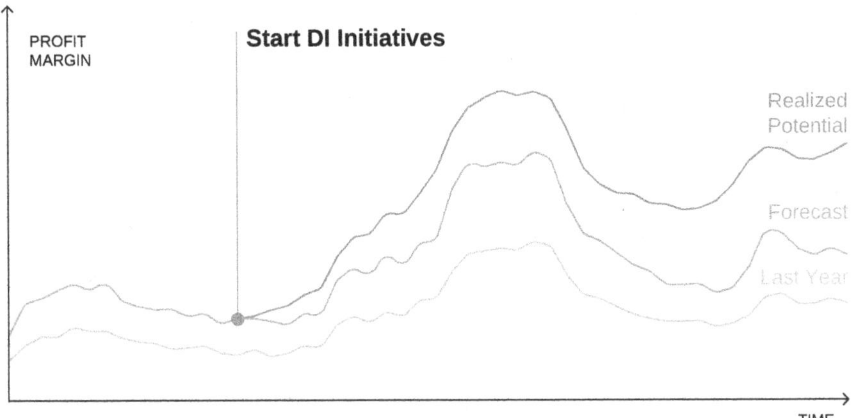

FIGURE 4.1 Client use-case: realized potential after the start of DI initiatives.

We will take a look into the engine room of DI in Chapter 7 to see how this is possible, but these benefits can add up to significant cost savings and the unlocking of entirely new potential within enterprise applications, which is not a one-time effect, but a recurring lever. In Figure 4.1 we see the leap in potential after the introduction of a DI tool and related measures over time.

Planning and Forecasting the Next Level

We've already introduced the idea that Decision Intelligence goes beyond business intelligence systems. DI is a much more holistic approach for organizations that focuses on the decision-making process itself, rather than just analyzing the data. A sound Decision Intelligence initiative thus helps to identify the actual problems and then solve them by transforming raw data gathered from various sources into actionable profit-making insights. In this sense, it's also taking a much more proactive approach to decision-making.

Rather than simply reacting to data and events as they occur, Decision Intelligence helps organizations anticipate and plan for potential future scenarios. This can involve using scenario planning and other forecasting techniques to identify potential risks and opportunities and developing contingency plans to mitigate risks and take advantage of opportunities. Very often, improved planning or smarter and better forecasting supported by machine learning is the first step to implement DI strategically in organizations, because at this point there is no need to change the process of decision-making; we "just" need to improve the accuracy of forecasting or make it more efficient (by reducing manual work) and dynamic (by shortening planning cycles).

Making Decisions at Scale: The Ultimate DecisionOS

There is an ultimate target picture (or vision) of a decision system fully integrated into organizational structure, processes, and operations, which we call decisionOS (a Decision Intelligence operating system). Think of it as a complex graph/map, a comprehensive digital twin of the enterprise, with all triggers, inputs, outputs, different levels of decision hierarchies, processes, and so on. Ultimately, we are left with a *system of systems*, where the organization acts as a large overarching system, and multiple subsystems with decision-making processes (such as supply chain optimization, or more tangible decisions like the "rebuy process" and other recurring choices) are interconnected. Everything is interrelated, and many subsystems, triggers, and decisions affect one another. Just as the inputs and outputs of the higher-level system "organization" are very sophisticated (resources, raw materials, lifetime), so are the outputs; ultimately, each system pays into the three Ps: people, planet, profit (although in our experience working with many organizations, the order and prioritization can vary). The subsystems, on the other hand, are more concrete, and it is easier to model the rebuy decision process because it is designed to reduce costs and prevent stockouts by predicting demand per product and region and managing inventory accordingly.

Marco Alberti, the founder of the renowned strategy and OKR consulting company MURAKAMY, worked with more than 100 companies on strategy and goalsetting and sees precisely in the management of the subsystems and the overarching system one of the central tasks of management to be and remain successful in the long term:

> *Accordingly, we have to create a balance and consider all these dimensions with their effects and their dependencies on each other . . . we must manage the contradictions and the conflicts and make them visible, to make them conscious, to decide actively and to endure . . . and that is . . . the task of the management of the future.*
>
> (Alberti, 2022)

Coming back to DI and the complexity of several use-cases, it becomes clear that it makes sense to start with one use-case at a time. Once this is successful (and in our experience this can take some time), it is much easier to introduce the DI approach to other departments and even to use it in multiple departments to realize its full potential. But just think of the enormous potential DI can have in your business!

Step up the Operational Game: Recurring Use-Cases for Companies

Having previously discussed the significance of deriving value from data strategically, the key question now is: where can this be used very concretely? There are many areas where DI can take a company to new heights and drive effective business growth. We have a lot of examples in various places throughout the book, so let's try a (certainly not exhaustive) list of key use-cases here.

1. **Generating customer growth:** Acquiring a new customer can be up to five times more expensive than retaining an existing one, making customer retention a top priority for many businesses. As a result, data-driven customer interaction has become increasingly important in recent years. Data science helps you to refine customer profiles and create more precise and effective marketing campaigns.

   By analyzing customer behavior, companies can use predictive and prescriptive analytics tools to identify customers who are more likely to make additional purchases, as well as those who may be considering switching to a competitor. The goal of data-driven customer analytics is to create a unified, accurate view of a company's customer base that can be used as a basis for making decisions about attracting and retaining future customers.

   On top of that, companies can identify high-value customers and recommend proactive ways to engage with them. Vandevelde (2021) has shown that customers who are targeted with personalized emails spend 38% more, and 70% of customers who are retargeted can be persuaded to stay loyal to your company.

   Loyal customers are essential to any business, and data science can be used to prevent churn. Reference cases from McKinsey, Mohr, and Hürtgen (2018) show that in a period of between one and three years, using data science can lead to a decrease of up to 10%. By using churn models to pinpoint the pain points, companies can fix problems in the customer journey way before they might result in lost customers.

2. **Increasing sales:** Use-cases of Decision Intelligence to increase sales typically help companies improve their customer-centric activities in the areas of pricing, cross-selling, upselling, and advertising optimization.

   In marketing, AI-based decision-making helps you to analyze past customer behavior and score leads, driving the company to greater sales efficiency. A potential customer leaves data on a website that can be used to gain important insights into consumer behavior and then a predictive model can be built from this information. Companies using artificial intelligence to evaluate leads have been proven to be able to make 50% more appointments and reduce calling time by 60% (Leong, 2019).

   For airlines focusing on price optimization, analysis has shown that the nearer customers can get to their desired departure date, the more they are willing to pay – even up to 50% more. This can also be applied to other industries by examining customer reactions to price changes using sentiment analysis, which can identify customers' reactions to a specific event on social media.

   Based on more than 100 reference cases in terms of top line use-cases (that is, revenue and gross sales), McKinsey et al. (2018) found that data-driven insights and decisions have an impact on growth by up to 2% in the areas of assortment optimization, cross-selling and upselling, pricing, inventory optimization, and shelf stocking.

3. **Reducing costs:** If you're looking to reduce costs, leveraging Decision Intelligence can make a significant impact. By using data-driven insights to optimize internal processes, you can unlock immense cost-saving potential and streamline operations, identify areas where processes can be made more

efficient, eliminate redundancies, and reduce waste, all of which can translate into cost savings for your organization.

Over a period of one to three years, McKinsey studied the impact of data science on net profit and concluded that when looking at bottom line use-cases, potential savings in expenses are hidden, including reduction of call center costs by 20% to 50% with predictive maintenance, up to 10% of marketing costs with higher effectiveness of expenses, up to 30% of inventory costs by improved demand planning, and up to 30% of logistics costs by optimization of supply chains.

When it comes to banking, Decision Intelligence approaches can be a game-changer in several ways as well. For instance, using time series analytics can help predict when customers are likely to be late with payments. By doing so, banks can take preemptive measures to prevent breaches of contract and defaults by offering timely support. This not only helps maintain a positive customer experience but also minimizes the risk of loss for the bank.

Another important area where DI can make a big difference is in fraud prevention. Banks can use a special DI-based software that helps them detect patterns and identify potential fraudsters to prevent fraud before it even happens. This is a win-win situation: the banks save money and also protect their customers' interests.

4. **Increase employee and customer satisfaction:** There are many use-cases in the customer experience space, given that we are all used to recommendations (both good and bad) when looking for the next product, movie, song, or restaurant. There are also many applications in customer service beyond the familiar chat bot; for example, we see great success with companies predicting service requests and optimizing their customer service accordingly. At the same time, in

most cases, a smoothly operating DI application leads to greater employee satisfaction because manual work is reduced and internal processes can run much smarter (The caveat here is a fear that this means jobs will be taken over by AI.)

5. **Support in meeting sustainability goals:** Finding optimized solutions in the supply chain or in manufacturing regarding sustainability by managing the costs can make a real difference. What we are seeing here in companies is that this topic is gaining in popularity, partly due to the "zeitgeist" and the will of managers, and partly due to regulation and transparency obligations. For example, a typical use-case here can be found in logistics: how to dynamically find good trade-off between CO_2 emissions, delivery capability (or customer satisfaction), and logistics costs on a daily basis.
6. **Manufacturing/shopfloor/IoT:** In manufacturing, production, and on the shopfloor, the opportunities for DI use-cases are exploding as various Internet of Things (IoT) sensors and other Industry 4.0 initiatives digitize nearly every machine and production process. In addition to inventory management and supply chain management, machine learning approaches can be used for production planning, root cause analysis, and quality control. The most common use-case is predictive maintenance. DI techniques can be used to analyze machine performance data and predict when maintenance is needed, reducing downtime and increasing machine availability.
7. **Internal (legal, HR, finance, etc.):** Of course, there are also various internal use-cases, such as recruitment in HR or financial forecasting, risk analysis, and fraud detection in finance. In legal, DI can be used to analyze large volumes of legal documents and contracts, helping lawyers identify important clauses, potential risks, and negotiation opportunities. There are many more possible applications, and here

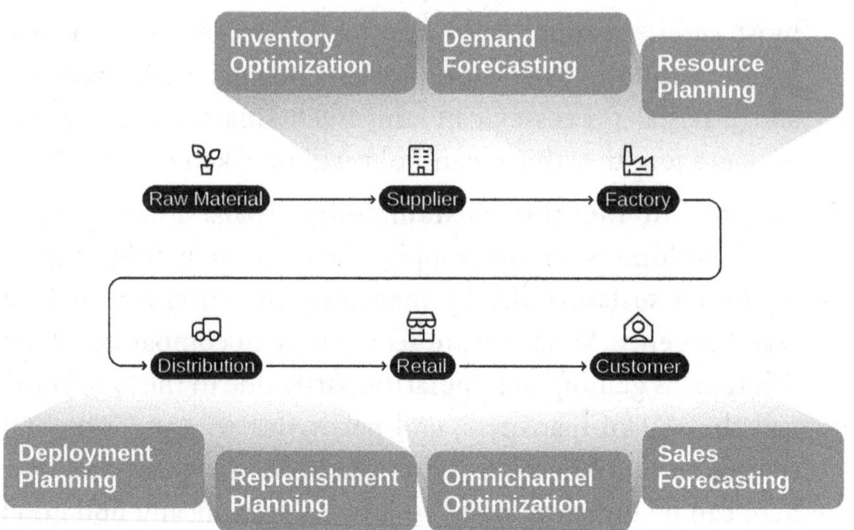

FIGURE 4.2 Example for use-cases along the value chain/supply chain.

the synergies with other technologies such as process mining are very promising.

As we have seen, there is almost no area in an organization where the intelligent combination of humans and machines is not an option for teams to become faster, find new alternatives, and adapt quickly to change. Or, to put it more drastically, due to increasing speed and complexity, as well as technological capabilities, Decision Intelligence is becoming an indispensable and crucial capability for companies. But what does this mean in detail for a specific use-case? Let's look at a few examples in the next chapter to see in detail how this is possible.

CHAPTER

5

Decision Intelligence in Practice: Industry Examples of Applied DI

"We do a lot of things in analyzing data and stuff, but we're just looking in the rearview mirror. I can't wait to take a look in the crystal ball!"

– An experienced manager from a big manufacturing company[1]

Data science and behavioural science barely know industry borders, since their possibilities are limitless, but the way these mechanisms are applied can differ depending on the industry and domain. This chapter serves as an inspiration for how to map the general techniques to your specific domain to take full advantage of Decision Intelligence in practice. For each industry, we focus on one of the problems with the biggest lever. Many problems described for one industry are also applicable to others because there is a high intersection between similar industries. Hold tight, and let's dive deeper into real-life applications of Decision Intelligence.

DI in Logistics

If you think planning a trip to multiple destinations is a headache, imagine figuring out the most efficient route for a salesperson to visit several clients while minimizing costs and travel time. This is the famous "traveling salesman problem," one of the best-known mathematical challenges.

But now, with the help of data and technology, logistics experts are tackling even more complex versions of this problem every day. Instead of just one salesperson, they are dealing with the challenge of shipping multiple products to various locations.

---

[1]This quote is from a manager we collaborated with on a data transformation project. Since then, we've used this analogy internally to illustrate the distinction between backward-looking data analytics tools and forward-looking methods in Decision Intelligence. But to be completely transparent, the crystal ball analogy is a highly controversial topic of debate among our data scientists.

If this doesn't sound like a big deal to you, remember that the devil lies in the detail, particularly as the number of possibilities grows exponentially.

To provide you with a clearer understanding of exponential growth, just try to estimate the number of times you must fold a paper (even if not physically feasible) in order to achieve a height that reaches the moon. Close your eyes for a minute and use your imagination to come up with a number.

Now let's unveil the magic number. You only need to fold the paper 42 times to surpass a height of 384.000 kilometers! So we see why many people tend to argue that 42 is the answer to all questions.[2]

Let's look at the math behind this phenomenon. Figure 5.1 illustrates the power of exponential growth. Initially, the first

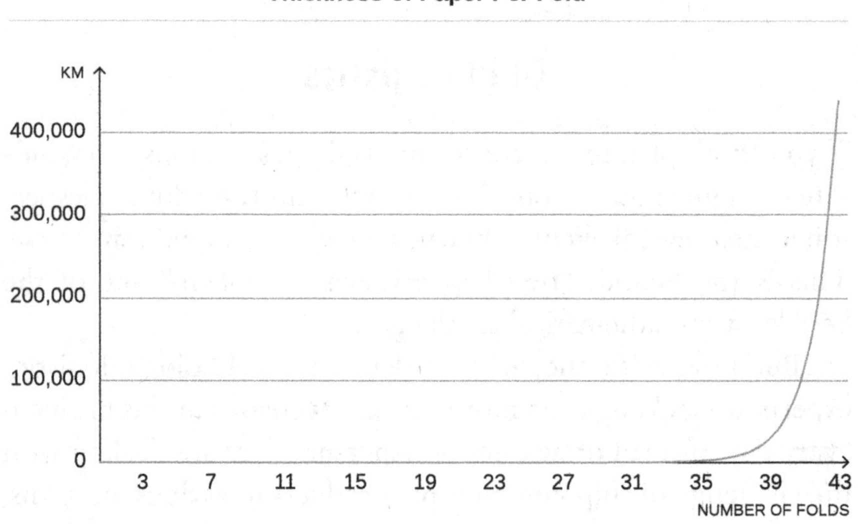

FIGURE 5.1 Thickness of paper per fold.

[2] This number plays a vital role in the fandom of science-fiction author Douglas Adams. In his book *The Hitchhiker's Guide to the Galaxy*, a super computer called Deep Thought is built specifically to determine the answer to "the Ultimate Question of Life, the Universe, and Everything."

36 folds appear to show no growth toward reaching the moon at 384,000 kilometers away. But with just 6 additional folds, the paper surpasses this distance by a wide margin. Each fold doubles the height, so that each step makes the size of the surface twice as large as it was before. This is one small example that demonstrates how hard it is for us to imagine exponential growth. Because human brains think in a linear way, we extrapolate linearly most of the time.

Let's go back to logistics and supply chain with this example in the back of our mind. As mentioned, the world of logistic and supply chain management faces an exponentially increasing number of potential solution scenarios, depending on an assortment of variable factors.

A common use-case is distributing articles between different warehouses to serve local stores (see Figure 5.2). Each warehouse can ship articles from one warehouse to another or directly to a store. Each warehouse can only ship one type of product at a time – let's say razor blades – which means it is not feasible to fulfill an order of 20 requested products from two or more different warehouses. To simplify this example, we won't assume

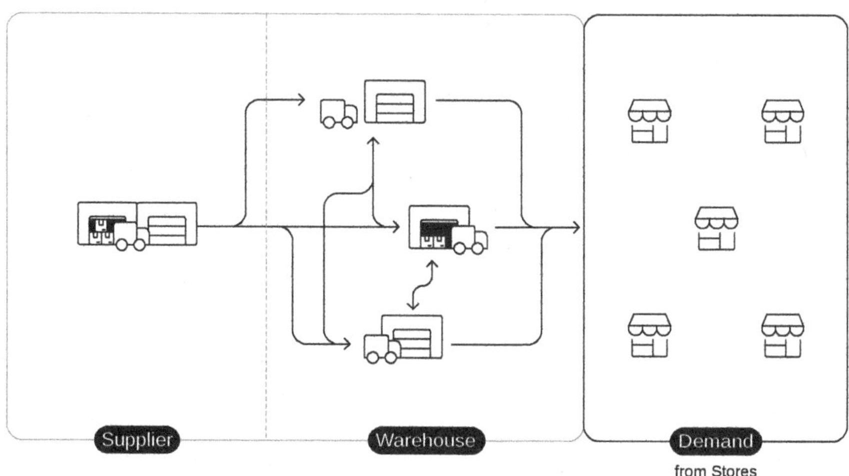

FIGURE 5.2 Schematic overview: warehouse scenario.

any further constraints. The number of potential options will depend on the total number of requested products per store and the number of available warehouses.

We will begin with a straightforward scenario featuring one warehouse and four requested products (razors, knives, forks, spoons), each with a quantity of 5000. Because there is only one warehouse, there are no alternatives and the number scenarios to fulfill the job equals 1. Consequently, the warehouse simply needs to check which articles are out of stock and order them from the central supplier.

Scenario	Warehouse 1
1	Razors, knives, forks, spoons

After several month of growing business, the fulfiller establishes a second warehouse. Our number of possible scenarios thus grows from 1 to 16. This table displays all possible options to illustrate how fast the solution space is growing.

Scenario	Warehouse 1	Warehouse 2
1	Razors, knives, forks, spoons	—
2	Razors, knives, forks	Spoons
3	Razors, knives, spoons	Forks
4	Razors, forks, spoons	Knives
5	Razors, knives	Forks, spoons
6	Razors, forks	Knives, spoons
7	Razors, spoons	Knives, forks
8	Razors	Knives, forks, spoons
9	Knives, forks, spoons	Razors
10	Knives, forks	Razors, spoons
11	Knives, spoons	Razors, forks
12	Knives	Razors, forks, spoons
13	Forks, spoons	Razors, knives
14	Forks	Razors, knives, spoons
15	Spoons	Razors, knives, forks
16	—	Razors, knives, forks, spoons

To keep this book below 1000 pages, we will not expand the detailed exercise further to cover business growth involving additional warehouses and perhaps even more items. Instead, let's dive deeper into the reasoning behind this logic. Mathematically we can calculate the number of possibilities this way:

$$Number\ of\ Warehouses^{Number\ of\ Articles}$$

With two warehouses and four articles we therefore get $2^4 = 2 \times 2 \times 2 \times 2 = 16$

Continuing down this path, the number of possible scenarios grows to 81 when adding a third warehouse. Now imagine that most fulfillment teams or companies deal with thousands of products rather than just four. To give you a real-life example of one of the companies we supported in their DI activities, a fulfiller handling the distribution of 10,000 products with three warehouses must choose between this many options (the equivalent of 3^{5000}):

40389976297871553397008634098150847783944981667759
76374862318662815021844263163724409589991283112221
95708703712726440925298211274859178771703383040344
19302831610118812904316419669806235690286648689627
02914864744551077531848115736772683548758847258321
09480816007929295655276317110406798412053383606566
46359502423649284424518059950783172484611404441399
95818842326862989533584638540917303432618956468436
26746221768989753693922153800868372159194612033353
21439178724491361481083725594912678867876393504325
67049929505139561975168349141248659914132248759237
99750541915947121452317397071057126304566886323132
37159379008214855068707296575317570265557373712948
25429353175800946829026948092511256737220542210787
05305159580298123310985601211352555250997323547989
79376955488078266328549362708476932055774657608390

5892281995269667652497312862937378619656482275464l
9290429591462439038555624893561619568785954l508269
2189276329429991504770124701085279239460876288448 7
4010913857489206276252114325178985606399745389659 2
2414444350837413079944180530897470116392449921436 1
7911287606647084965258198883225653388806207929500 3
3223059418285493291048089968257520004746863136622 4
7561846712056877773557913094816647522057377238276 0
5017299803707184630307441302672768508598302249090 4
5374931284637548474276339644646276078922281764529 2
6495692268689787553685528221749101480148463277422 1
8968086229060583051969616187683845992803504299049 6
0585449130847220261622518858769620805308646320741 3
2617826126984984843534068119465923915208768348376 8
1364361483077335648507177704989176676017490814214 1
5494578545630706744480882869969744817804435874448 6
1500761152862584694865134020872483840686556581145 1
8474837867145754599634609879861608173455937726377 2
5343784722309807229968176006683894290612608864774 1
1191414145524898862895682862959613387393885921344 5
8987217604566798319860335993725331565539619297067 0
4163556063532953648893078691339202625369223335024 1
0453259996435324688249532943706881660939492788636 6
4041795436910656750167596038501554362222214884786 8
7039354514457890619044805913468089164536163934700 0
2327191538866788365255688115338002309292544972383 1
4075866436365607455976085809437067430000427425918 3
0363857026327767857873259045370091838668027782700 5
0165881888847305210455149967088362881806347999559 1
1110684992623893342705163686819347170019922026233 2
0857716933794168735052645498039818859137502378346 8
711359732633600493563136998276100001

Just for reference, this number is larger than the number of stars in the universe.

Imagine stepping into the role of a fulfiller: The main objective is to reduce transportation expenses while simultaneously optimizing inventory levels and ensuring product availability. In today's world, Excel is a widely used tool to navigate many options and find a workable solution. However, considering the intricate complexity, shifting dynamics, constraints, and various dependencies in real-life situations, one might wonder why Excel is still the most commonly used tool for tackling such challenges.

Of course, there are many digital logistics tools to address this challenge, but to really take this case to the next level, we need to understand how to approach it in a different way. First, it is important to connect and structure the data and the business problem. In Chapter 6, we will take a closer look at why this is so important and how it works. For now, we'll stick with the result, a so-called causal diagram, which shows the business logic, the data points, and the interconnected various triggers from inputs to output. It is also possible to add constraints to mirror the given business problem as much as possible. (See an example of a causal diagram in Figure 6.8.)

The new order quantities are determined based on sales and the existing stock levels. How the articles are ordered to and from different warehouses will lead to different costs and availabilities. Decision intelligence uses the causal diagram to simulate different scenarios and their outcomes: "What happens when I order three products from warehouse 1 and the other products from warehouse 3?"

But instead of giving the user just the simulation model (equivalent to what was already available in Excel without predictive data), the huge solution space is boiled down in an efficient way with AI-based optimization. These methods had their roots at NASA, where every experiment involved a lot of resources and therefore optimization had to be accurate.

As a result, the user gets a simple list with one or few optimal scenarios of how to order different articles.

Optimal Scenario	Warehouse 1	Warehouse 2	Costs	Avg. Stock Coverage
1	100 razors 200 spoons	50 knives 50 forks	20.000	3 weeks
2	200 razors	50 knives 50 forks 50 spoons	23.000	4 weeks

Compared to the complicated Excel table, this has one huge advantage: the scenarios are based on finished solutions. The human is put into the driver seat again and can compare the scenarios to each other to see which one is better for the current situation of the company instead of trying out a few different Excel scenarios until one is found to fulfill the given requirements.

Another widely used application of DI in logistics is to determine the number of drivers needed, or rather the optimal number of drivers for shipping and fulfilling existing orders. The problem that many companies delivering goods face is easy to grasp: if too many vehicles with respective drivers are booked, all packages can perfectly be distributed fast, but this comes with high costs and high CO_2 emissions. When fewer drivers are booked, the costs go down, but the service level may also decrease.

At first this seems straightforward, but as in the use-case above, the details matter. Some dimensions and constraints increase the complexity. Most logistic fulfillers have more than one fulfilment center for which this problem needs to be solved, so the sheer number alone increases the complexity (remember, the number of options grows exponentially). On the other hand, the costs increase extremely for the booking of additional

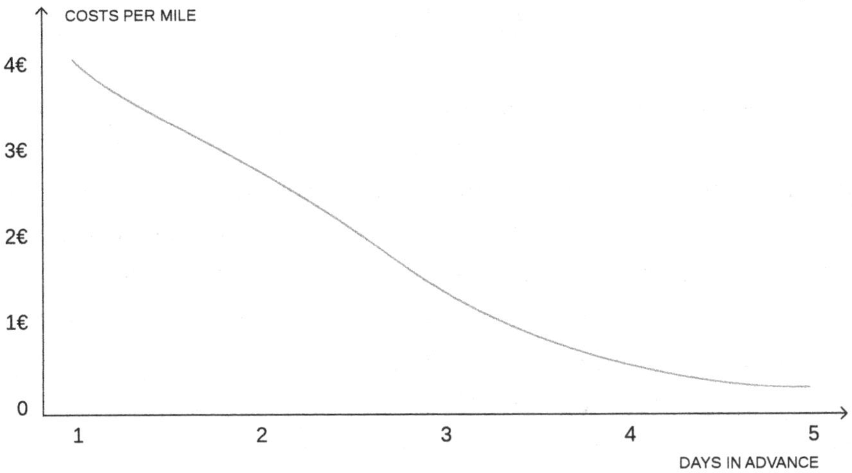

FIGURE 5.3 The effect of short-term bookings on costs per mile.

vehicles and drivers who have to be rebooked at short notice on the day of operation (as depicted in Figure 5.3).

As a result, dynamic changes of information require fast changes of the situation in order to minimize additional costs. Let's imagine the optimization normally runs six days in advance to staff drivers and vehicles. One core part is a prediction of how many parcels are expected to be delivered. The prediction now changes three days before the planned date due to a change in expected behavior. A new optimization is required to find out the optimal number of drivers and vehicles and – as we saw in the previous figure – it is still less expensive to react now than waiting for the day itself. Handling such constantly changing systems requires a Decision Intelligence system. This enables monitoring and detecting changes fast and gives updated recommendations to reach the defined service level. In comparison to the status quo, it puts the user in an active role rather than having to react at the last moment on the delivery date.

DI in Retail

The retail industry is one of the most dynamic and wide-ranging fields and generates massive amounts of data on consumer behavior, sales, inventory, and supply chain operations. At the same time, this industry is both affected by and dependent on many other industries, which is one of the reasons it has become so advanced in terms of data collection and usage. The main objective is to sell as many products as possible with strong unit economics. To achieve this goal, there are many different ways to use Decision Intelligence:

- Pricing
- Discounting and markdown
- Product placements and target audiences
- Rebuy
- Replenishment

In today's uncertain times, one of the most critical issues to address is having the right articles at the right place at the right time, because this guarantees maximum sales while keeping logistic costs low. This implies focusing on shipping the necessary items to the stores that need them. Achieving this optimal state requires many informed decisions at various points in time. There are two main questions requiring more intelligence to answer optimally:

- Rebuy: How many articles need to be ordered or rebought from which supplier?
- Replenishment: How are the warehouses replenished based on the given orders?

The following sections explore how DI can help to find good answers to those questions in a reasonable amount of time. As for any good decision-making process, the key starting points are problem definition and stakeholder management.

Let's look at the problem and the stakeholders involved – mainly two stakeholder groups with different needs. On one side is a manager responsible for establishing departmental goals to improve overall company objectives. On the other side are operative analysts striving to meet the manager's requirements and objectives. Both stakeholders face individual challenges to find an optimal solution, which we will elaborate on further as we define the problem later.

The manager typically has two goals, each driven by two risks that need to be minimized:

1. The risk of running out of stock due to ordering too little, which results in lost sales
2. The risk of ordering too much of a specific article that isn't in high demand, resulting in higher logistic costs, lost revenue, and possibly even the need for massive discounts or product disposal

The primary lever to minimize the risk and steer the targets is:

The number of orders of different products / SKUs

(SKU = stock keeping unit, a unique number given to an article or product so that it can be clearly identified and tracked)

The complexity here is that there are many different products available, which makes it difficult to manage and align them all. Plus, it's tough to predict how demand will change for each product, so it's almost impossible for a human to solve this problem in the best possible way.

So what can a solution look like?

DI is the perfect assistant to embrace complexity and put the manager and the analyst into the driver seat by:

- *Predicting* future demand and sales based on the data
- *Determining the optimal number of orders* per product to find the right balance between minimizing costs and risks while maximizing availability to reduce lost sales opportunities

To make a *sales prediction*, the analyst provides input on factors that impact future sales in addition to historical sales. These factors can differ between retailers, but commonly include events like holidays, promotions, and discounts for specific products.

To find the *optimal number of orders*, the problem is modeled in a causal way, as already shown in the problem definition. At this part, both the analysts and the manager play a critical role because they have an immense amount of knowledge. The causal diagram basically makes their implicit decision logic and process explicit. By using the predicted proxy for future sales and existing stock levels, orders for different products are set. The logistics costs and availability levels can then be calculated, including specific constraints such as transportation time from fulfillers to the warehouse or batch sizes for different products.

Because most of the processes are still highly manual and error-prone, automating the causal problem can provide a significant value for the analyst. The key is to represent the problem from a problem-oriented perspective rather than different silos with high-maintenance interfaces. This approach results in the operative analyst receiving only relevant information required for making decisions. For example, in the rebuy case, the number of orders for each SKU is displayed along with context information like the current stock level, predicted sales, and optimization targets. Instead of now merging different Excel tables and exports from ERP software and a data warehouse, such as SAP or Snowflake, all necessary information is readily available to the decision-maker responsible for execution as the data layer is connected upfront to a Decision Intelligence tool.

As we discussed earlier, now the company can decide about the automation level of the system. The decision can be augmented by the analyst checking the decision table on a daily basis and acting accordingly. In the next step, these decision tables can also be fully automated and only need to be supervised by the analyst once enough trust has been established.

The manager, on the other hand, gains transparent insights into various scenarios and the trade-offs involved in achieving the company targets. This allows them to guide their organization based on actual outcomes. Each trade-off point corresponds to a scenario that determines the operative outcomes of the tables mentioned earlier.

Before and during the pandemic, many retailers had a primary focus on growth at any cost. However, this approach has shifted toward a more sustainable growth mindset. This shift in mindset usually takes a while and involves a lot of talking, but Decision Intelligence tools make it a lot easier because the teams can see the different scenarios and so are able to react much faster to new strategic directions. In Figure 5.4 we see an example of a trade-off view with different outcomes (regarding the target KPIs "logistic costs" and "availability"). Now the manager and the respective teams can choose the best possible decision given the market demands and internal strategies. One game changer with this approach is that the decision-maker gets transparency on optimal solutions.

In the trade-off view, it becomes clear that there are also many suboptimal scenarios which often are the default scenario in which many companies operate (more details can be found in Chapter 7). Once a decision on the trade-off scenario has been

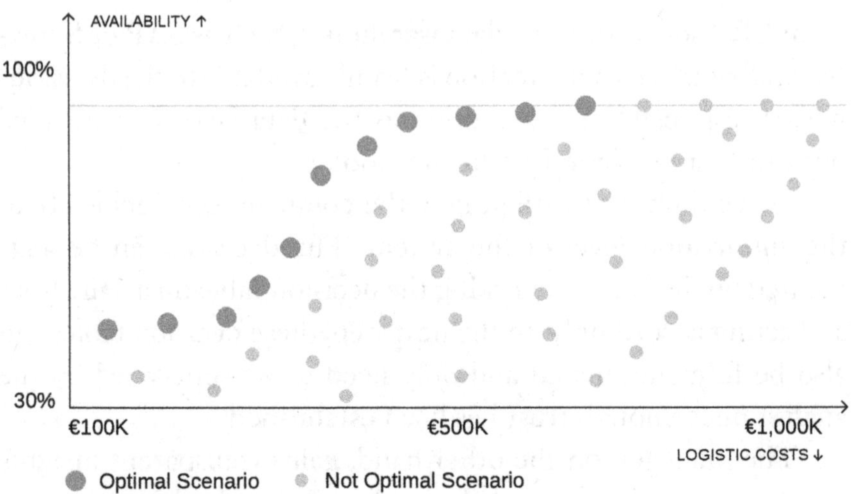

FIGURE 5.4 Trade-off view with optimal solutions for two targets.

set between the different target KPIs, the manager can lean back until another change in tactics is required. The operative implications will meanwhile be directly translated into the daily operations and be considered when generating new decision recommendations (see Figure 5.5).

After implementing a DI logic and system for this use-case, different stakeholders can benefit from that solution and adjacent use-cases can be addressed. As we will see in later, when we take a look at the engine of DI systems, the company is also able to react much faster to change (for example, by retraining

Recommended Orderlist

SKU	Status	Further Orders from Supplier (Recommendation)	Already Ordered (Not Arrived Yet)	Current Stock Level	Predicted Sales	Availability Next Month without Reordering
12313131	understocked	3,800	300	1,700	4,500	44 %
4291310	overstocked	0	0	1,370	1,100	100 %
3131931	good	1,200	100	1,900	2,300	80 %

FIGURE 5.5 Example of order list recommendations.

models) and connect different use-cases in different silos throughout the company.

DI in Pricing and Marketing

For many companies, data-driven acquisition of customers is the key lever for running a successful business. Understanding how and where to acquire the right customers at the right cost should by no means be seen as just a way of making your marketing run more efficiently; it can also have a significant impact on the long-term success of your business. To give you an example, if you are running an e-commerce business and looking to attract customers who are likely to make repeat purchases, you can significantly improve your unit economics. The key lies in accurately predicting the lifetime value (LTV) of your customers and targeting those with a high LTV.

The economic crisis has triggered a shift in focus from growth-only metrics to a more holistic approach in customer acquisition. Many companies that once prioritized growth at any cost are realizing the importance of balancing acquisition strategies with both growth and profitability now. Those that can strategically balance the two will come out on top in this era.

To achieve this balance, Decision Intelligence approaches must be a pillar. Let's dive into two specific applications of these tools in the B2C sector: dynamic pricing on price-comparison websites and budget mix optimization for direct digital acquisition.

Dynamic Pricing on Price-Comparison Websites

In business areas with a high number of competing offers, price-comparison websites (PCWs) are incredibly useful because they enable users to easily compare offers across the market and choose the one that suits their needs best. Over the past few years, PCWs have gained a significant market share in a variety of industries, including flights, hotels, financial services, utilities, and various consumer goods.

Typically, PCWs offer a search interface as their entry point, where users input their preferences and receive a ranked list of quotes relevant to their search. When it comes to conversion, data confirm a behavior you probably intuitively guessed: conversion rates are heavily correlated to the quote's rank on the list. This means that the higher your quote ranks, the better your chances of getting clicked on and chosen by a user.

Sure, there are many second-order effects like brand awareness, brand reputation, and customer reviews that can impact your success, but the biggest factor is where your quote ranks. And you know what affects your ranking position the most? Your price! Of course, there are other second-order and PWC-specific ranking factors that matter too, but ultimately price is king. So here's a simple rule when it comes to price elasticity on PCWs: if your price for a specific user request is lower than your competitors' cheapest offer, your product is more likely to get chosen by a user. But if your price is higher, they'll probably go with someone else. It's a simple rule, but mastering it is anything but easy!

Imagine a utilities company that's trying to sell electricity contracts on a PCW. Typically, they'll need to consider factors like zip code, yearly consumption, payment cycle, and minimum contract length. Even though this might not seem like a lot, all these parameters can combine in over a million different ways to create unique quote configurations. To give you another example, if you search for a new home insurance you might need to enter more than 25 parameters to configure your quote, and this easily results in more than a billion possible quote configurations.

Mastering the simple pricing rule we talked about earlier is nearly impossible if you are trying to figure out the best prices for every single possible product configuration manually. And if that's not difficult enough, you will most likely encounter two additional challenges: the incomplete market data, and the constantly changing markets. So even if you somehow manage to perfect your pricing strategy after spending weeks crunching data in Excel, chances are it'll be outdated as soon as you implement it and won't even get you the results you wanted.

So let's say you had access to a system that constantly provides you with the prices of all competitors at a PCW. What would be a sound pricing strategy? Just keep undercutting the cheapest competitor for every potential user quote? Sure, that might get you lots of new customers, but your CFO might start asking some tough questions about whether it's actually making you any money. This is a classic trade-off scenario between growth and profitability that you should be aware of when trying to acquire new customers on PCWs.

Modern decision-augmenting dynamic pricing solutions use the most high-tech forecasting and optimization technologies to deal with these challenges. They basically do all the hard work and help companies adjust their pricing strategies dynamically, so they get the best possible results across all their PCW distribution channels.

Taking all the above considerations into account, successful dynamic pricing solutions combine all of the following components:

1. **Third-party and custom market data integration:** There are multiple ways to integrate market data on competitor prices for specific PCWs. What data is available can differ quite drastically across products, industries, and PCWs, from only a few hundred datapoints available through third-party

data platforms up to daily full data available through an API offered by the PCW itself. Good solutions offer a range of data integration possibilities and third-party integration out of the box.

2. **Market/competition price forecast capabilities:** Given the price sensitivity mechanics of PCWs, knowing about competitor prices and quote volumes is a key piece of information. Good solutions leverage the latest machine learning technology to provide accurate competitor forecasts on a per-quote level and quote volumes based on the available market data.
3. **LTV data and custom model integration:** As pointed out above, if you only optimize for the market, you would over-optimize on growth and neglect profitability. Good solutions allow you to add company internal data sources and even company internal models to integrate to predicted lifetime value of every acquired contract setting optimal prices. If you don't have good LTV models available, a good first step is often to take an LTV proxy such as contract margin.
4. **Multi-objective optimization:** Good solutions allow you to actively steer the trade-off between optimizing for growth versus optimizing for LTV per acquired contract.

In a dynamic pricing application, there is a causal relationship between the different components. Usually everyone aims at maximizing the number of sold contracts and getting the highest average margin per contract. If you're trying to maximize both the number of contracts sold and the average margin per contract sold, you'll eventually reach a point where the channel manager has to balance growth and profitability. It is no luck that the top-notch solutions out there can show the channel manager all the possible pricing strategies and the trade-offs between them, in order for them to make an informed and

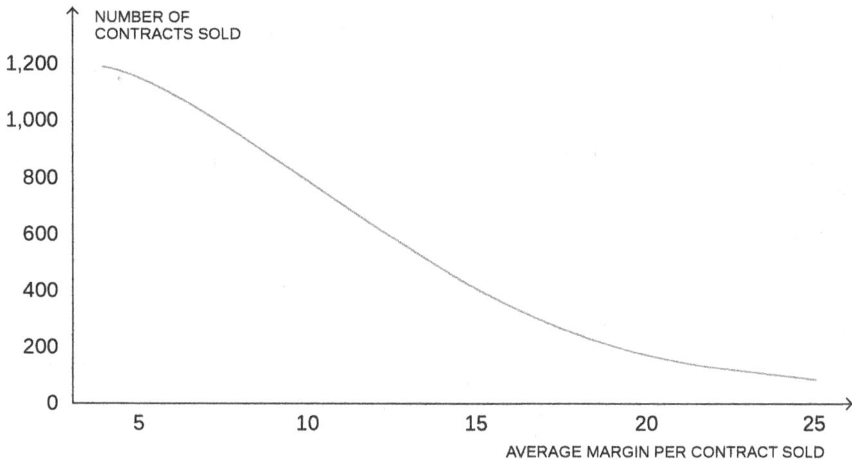

FIGURE 5.6 Example trade-off view for a channel manager.

optimal decision every time – not one based only on gut feeling as we mentioned before.

Figure 5.6 shows what an exemplary decision trade-off view for a channel manager might look like. Basically, each point on the decision curve represents a possible optimal pricing model, meaning it is a potential sweet spot for pricing that meets your business targets. The channel manager doesn't need to be a pricing whiz; they just need to choose an overall pricing strategy that aligns with their goals. The machine does all the magic in the background, and the results are easy to understand, not only for a tech person but also for the business manager and marketeer.

Dynamic Pricing for Other Channels

The core ideas outlined above can be applied for building decision-augmenting dynamic pricing applications for non-PCW acquisition channels as well. The key difference you will have to take into account is that the simple price sensitivity rule of PCWs won't be applicable to most other sales channels.

For example, consider the task of setting optimal prices for electricity contracts sold on your own utility company's website. When a user requests a quote, they are likely in some way or other comparing offers to make a decision. But, in contrast to PCWs, it's not at all clear what the user is using to compare your offer. There are many unknown variables involved in understanding price sensitivity. While you can make educated guesses and manually supplement your analysis with research data, the most effective approach to build a successful dynamic pricing strategy for other channels typically involves incorporating automated experiments and learning.

We also have thoroughly explored and tested how DI technology can be leveraged to dynamically set optimal pricing strategies. However, for direct acquisition channels, setting prices is just one component of the equation. If there is no demand for your products, you don't need to care about setting correct prices at all. Additionally, if you are attracting a large number of people with low interest in your product, prices become less significant, as you will not successfully acquire new customers. We will delve into how DI technology can also provide a solution to this problem in the next chapter.

Budget Mix Optimization for Direct Acquisition

In B2C companies, the marketing budget is one of the biggest cost factors for their profit and loss (P&L). The key challenge for marketeers is to spend each marketing dollar as efficiently as possible. Over the past two decades, digital marketing has been the solution to this challenge. For each penny they spent on channels like Facebook and Google Ads, marketeers have been able to track its impact and optimize how they spent their next penny accordingly.

This approach works well as long as you can track user behavior across all digital touchpoints. Unfortunately, the cookie has started to crumble. Privacy-intrusive tracking technology has raised concerns among consumers, leading governments and major tech companies like Apple to impose legal restrictions and technological barriers. As a result, measuring the effectiveness of marketing might go back to the way it was before we had digital ad platforms.

The good news for marketeers is that, while tracking technology is becoming less reliable, AI is gaining traction and offering a solution. By using state-of-the-art machine learning technology, models learn how every dollar spent impacts business outcomes simply based on aggregate spend and transaction data, without the need to track and store individual user actions. With the help of this technology, powerful Decision Intelligence applications can be built, enabling marketeers regain the upper hand and optimize their marketing spends to meet their targets.

A typical setup of a decision model here takes *spend* and *sales* data from all the available marketing channels and uses machine learning models to predict each channel's saturation behavior. Then it adds factors like business-specific action days, seasonality data, and an internal LTV model that is used by the company to predict the future total revenue and ROI per customer.

Using multi-objective optimization technologies, modern DI applications can simulate how millions of different budget-channel-mix scenarios will impact the targets, giving the marketeer a transparent choice on how to optimally allocate their marketing dollars (see Figure 5.7). Figure 5.8 offers a glimpse of a Decision Intelligence tool marketeers can use for their daily work.

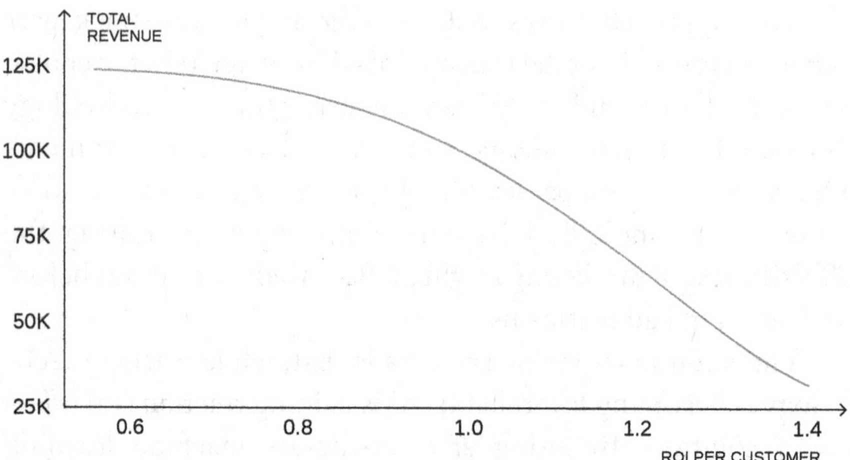

FIGURE 5.7 Optimized trade-offs for budget channel mix.

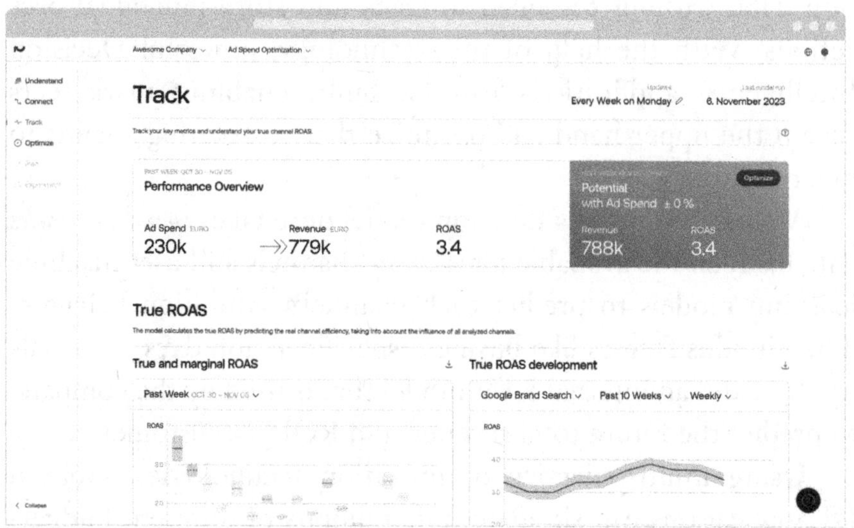

FIGURE 5.8 Example dashboard view of a Decision Intelligence platform (paretos).

After this deep dive into a few selected cases, we are confident that your imagination for specific use-cases is accelerated. We are breaking through "the rest is magic" ceiling and will now look into the machine room of Decision Intelligence.

CHAPTER

6

The Technology Stack: Applying AI Systems for Decision-Making

"Artificial intelligence is no magic, it's just math."

– Alan Turing

You might think this chapter would be another complicated technical section in a business book, making it hard to find helpful information for sound business and organizational choices. But we're taking a different approach. Our goal is to make this chapter easy to understand and helpful. This chapter offers the fundamental technical knowledge decision-makers need to create a successful data-driven organization. A basic understanding is crucial, with technology-driven intelligence being key to Decision Intelligence. This allows you to confidently question technical decisions and ensure they're right for moving your organization forward. It also helps you grasp what's possible and what's not, a vital skill for decision-makers in today's data organizations. Without this knowledge, the gap between decision-makers and those implementing solutions may continue to grow.

To succeed in a fast-changing world, it is key to always have access to the right information in its latest version. If you don't have good information, the technology you use basically doesn't matter. Data (=Information) forms the foundation for leveraging business value and determines the output generated by technology. In other words, poor quality data leads to poor results. Or as the machine learning community loves to say: "Shit in, shit out." Apart from the data quality, it's also vital to have access to it beyond silos and be able to aggregate it flexibly. That's the fertile soil to building a strong foundation for any successful business in the 21st century.

One of the most powerful applications that can be derived from this rich foundation is predictive AI technology. It is the next progressive step toward maximizing business value and shifting from a retrospective approach to a forward-looking perspective. And not only that, but it also enables cross-functional collaboration between otherwise siloed teams, enhancing planning capabilities, and boosting their overall efficiency. This is especially crucial nowadays because making predictions requires too much manual effort and expertise. AI algorithms can quickly learn complex patterns and respond effectively to changes in the environment and their impact on the organization.

The last step to unlock the full potential of decision-making is to shift AI algorithms from a passive role to an active one within the organization. It is enabled by implementing optimization methods, which work best once the other two technology topics are in place. With optimization technology, decision-making becomes resilient, and quick iterations enable optimal reactions. Instead of just presenting information, the algorithms provide clear recommendations for optimal scenarios and actions. This minimizes lost opportunities caused by suboptimal decisions. Optimizers are highly effective in exploiting millions of different scenario alternatives and identifying the best one for a given situation. In the past, such a process would have taken weeks or even months, but now, changes due to external factors or a shift in strategy can be reassigned within days or even hours.

When applied correctly, the combination of these three key technologies can have a massive business impact. As shown in Figure 6.1, these technologies are interdependent, and apart from data technology, they cannot generate significant business value on their own. Similar patterns can be observed in technology fields like process mining or RPA. In the following pages, we will delve deeper into each layer and explore what is necessary to ensure success.

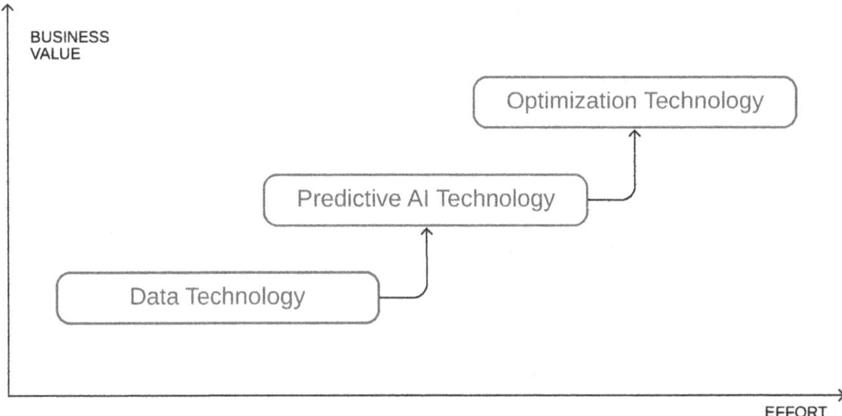

FIGURE 6.1 Effort and impact of implementing different technologies within a business.

Data, the Backbone to Leverage Business Value

Data is the raw information or facts that a computer system processes, and it can come in many forms such as numbers, text, images, audio, and video. Data can be used to make decisions, draw conclusions, and support communication and collaboration. In other words, anything we can sense as humans can be quantified as data. As technology advances in all areas (for example, sensor or software technology), the amount of collected data grows exponentially.

The good news is that collecting data will become less of a problem. However, the bad news is that it will become more challenging to obtain useful data in the right abstraction to benefit business users and applications. Moreover, updating and maintaining the data to ensure quality will also become more difficult. To overcome the challenges, it's important that you have a good data ontology, maintain a high data maturity, and use the right tools.

Data Ontology: Context Is King

The interpretation of a word or situation can differ based on one's background and context. For instance, when someone talks about "putting all their eggs in one basket," most people will understand it as an idiom cautioning against investing all resources in one place or depending too much on one plan. However, others unfamiliar with the idiom might imagine someone actually placing all their eggs in a single basket, which could lead to confusion. This difference in understanding could be due to cultural disparities or varied life experiences. Ultimately, an individual's perspective influences how they perceive things. Misinterpretations stemming from idiomatic expressions serve as some of the most tangible examples of this phenomenon. The most tangible examples are optical illusions. You probably know the famous one shown in Figure 6.2. What do you see in the picture? Depending on your background and perspective, you might see an elderly woman or a young woman.

The same can happen when different people look at the same data. It might seem as if they are talking about different things, when in many cases they are not. That's where data ontology comes in. It's a method to put the data into context by defining the properties of a subject area and how they are related to each other. One of the major tasks is to define how different pieces of data are related to each other. Figure 6.3 highlights this difference. If you just had data on profit, revenue, and cost, they could mean many different things, the same as if you don't know how they relate to one another or if you miss certain meta information. But if you add more information, like knowing that the profit is before taxes, everything becomes much clearer. It might seem like a small thing, but if people don't understand

FIGURE 6.2 Ambiguous picture of a young woman and an old woman.

each other when talking about data and if the information is not clear and transparent, it can become a huge deal and lead to fatal misunderstandings.

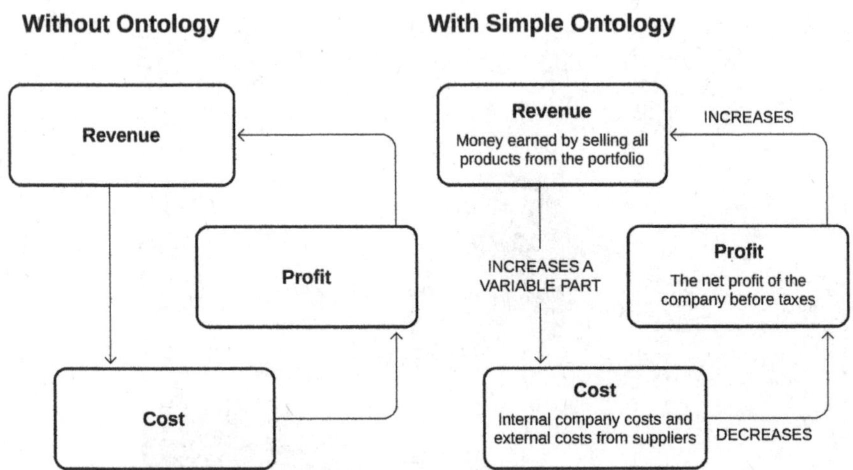

FIGURE 6.3 Example of a representation without and with ontology of interacting parameters.

A good data ontology helps to create a digital twin representation (i.e. a virtual replica) of the company to ensure that everyone is aligned on the data they look at and make it easier to search for the right data. As seen in the examples of DI in application in Chapter 5, modeling the given problem in a causal diagram with the idea of data ontology, meaning definition, constraints, and causal links, is a great foundation to automate a supported decision-making process. In most of the Decision Intelligence tools this is possible to visualize (see the causal diagram in Figure 6.8). If you want to dive deeper into the world of cause and effect, we highly recommend *The Book of Why* by Judea Pearl and Dana Mackenzie. It's an amazing ride through the "ladder of causation" and – while it's not an easy read – it comes with many nice examples as well: "If we are correct in our causal belief about aspirin the 'outcome' variable will respond by changing from 'headache' to 'no headache.' But no experiment and no AI can answer the question 'What would have happened if I had not taken the aspirin'" (Pearl & Mackenzie, 2019). And by the way, this perfectly describes a huge challenge of measuring effect of DI initiatives.

Data Maturity: Good Things Take Time (or at Least Effort)

In our experience, business users often say things like, "I'm not sure if I have enough data for AI." But here's the thing about this myth: the pure amount of data says almost nothing about whether AI or other methods can solve your problem and leverage your business's value. First of all, it depends on the specific question being asked and the available technologies to address it. So instead of saying, "I don't know if I have enough data for this," a better question might be, "Do I have the right data to solve my problem?" This revised statement shows that data quantity isn't everything. Other important factors include data diversity, quality, availability, and flexibility, which together define an organization's **data maturity**.

Let's look at these five factors of data maturity in more detail:

1. *Do we have enough relevant data?*

   Size still matters. When talking about **data quantity**, we are basically talking about the pure size of the available datasets. In other words: how much data do we have to work with? You can increase this score by increasing the number of data points within a specified time interval, or by looking at a bigger time frame. That second one has a massive influence on this score because it allows us to consider cyclical factors when we're making predictions. A good rule of thumb is to ask yourself, "How much more data do I have for the task I want to perform?" For example, if you're trying to predict something 10 days in advance, you'll want to have at least

15–30 times the amount of data you need for each aspect you are trying to predict.

2. *Do the relevant data sets have sufficient quality?*

   Data quality describes how good the data is – how well it's maintained, and how complete it is. Among other things, one of the checks is how many empty entries exist, whether all data comply with a certain type and format, and whether they are up-to-date. As a rule of thumb, less than 2% of your data in the existing data set should fall into one of the above categories.

3. *Do we have the relevant data points or inputs?*

   Data diversity measures the quantity of different relevant input sources of information (i.e. how many different sources your dataset is based on). For example, you can enrich your dataset with time-based, company internal, and third-party information to make sure you're finding the correct drivers for your target values. However, evaluating the *quality* of the input data and sources for a specific problem is not easy and can be indicated best by asking domain experts whether they think all the relevant information is available in the form of data. To get an even better idea, you will need to train prediction models and see how well they perform and then iterate by adding more inputs. Think of the ice cream example. If you as the owner of a café want to predict the demand for ice cream, it is obvious to consider the "weather" as a data input. But the particular day of the week, the vacation season, or competitors' prices can also affect demand for your business.

4. *Is the data available and always up to date?*

   Data availability indicates how much time and effort it takes to access the data and refers to both static data as well as data that is being updated regularly. This part is particularly important as poor data accessibility creates barriers to using data to solve problems. It is also one of the main causes for slow change and reluctance to initiate data-driven projects. To assess data availability, you can simply check how long it will take to obtain a dump of all relevant data without additional aggregations. If it takes more than two hours of human work, it is a sign of poor data availability. Later in a running data initiative it also considers the freshness – so in the best case, all data sources are connected and updated automatically.

5. *Can we use the data in a meaningful way and transform it for the given use-case?*

   Data flexibility refers to the ease of structuring the given data. Just because the data is available, it's not implied that it is available in the right format. Just think of terabytes of data produced by a plane during a flight. Although the raw data is available, it may not be useful. Identifying the right level of aggregation from scratch may take days. On the other hand, if the data has a logical structure with good references, it allows for fast and easy aggregation at different levels. Therefore, there are so many data lake and data warehouse initiatives in companies. But to reiterate: this is only one part of the game and should be executed in a very goal-oriented way. A data lake alone does not bring actionable insights.

   Like data availability, you can assess how well your organization is doing by checking how much time it takes to transform the available data into a particular aggregation format. For instance, if you have hourly raw data that includes sales for all products, and you need to calculate monthly sales for specific products, how long does it take to convert the data?

To evaluate each of these factors for your organization depends highly on your industry and the specific problems you want to solve. In general, it is advisable to focus on the most relevant and urgent problems facing your organization first. You can use the five categories and respective questions to evaluate the data maturity whenever you start (or think you are about to start) a Decision Intelligence initiative.

Artificial Intelligence: Understanding the Patterns Behind

Now let's move on to that magic ingredient of modern decision approaches and recommendation engines: artificial intelligence (AI). And what a time to be alive – we can ask an AI model itself for a definition. According to ChatGTP:[1]

> Artificial Intelligence (AI) is a cutting-edge field of computer science that involves the development of algorithms and systems capable of simulating human-like cognitive abilities, such as learning, problem-solving, and decision-making. These systems leverage vast amounts of data to identify patterns and make predictions, using techniques such as machine learning and neural networks, which are inspired by the human brain's structure and function. AI applications can optimize business processes, enhance customer experiences, and drive innovation across various industries by automating tasks, analyzing data, and providing intelligent recommendations. One key aspect of AI is its ability to improve over time through continuous learning, adapting to new information and refining its performance, leading to increased efficiency and accuracy. As AI continues to

[1] On April 16, 2023, we gave Open AI ChatGPT-4 this prompt: "Please give me a five-sentence definition of AI for a book aimed at business users who are curious about innovation, giving hints about the underlying functionality."

evolve, it offers businesses a competitive advantage by enabling them to harness the power of data-driven insights, automate routine tasks, and explore innovative solutions to complex challenges.[2]

Interestingly, this science in itself is not a very new development at all. Even before the age of computers, a machine called Mechanical Turk played its first chess games autonomously – until it eventually turned out that there was obviously a professional chess player hiding deep inside the machine.[3] Since the dawn of the principles of the modern computer, the idea of "machine intelligence" (later called "artificial intelligence") has been a topic of interest for scientists. Alan Turing himself wrote the first simple algorithm for playing chess in 1950; he even had to try it out on paper because the hardware wasn't ready. Dietrich Prinz managed to implement a simple chess algorithm on the first commercial computer Ferranti Mark 1 one year later. At the same time, science fiction books and movies frequently picked up the theme of artificial intelligence and shaped the image and imagination, and with the further development of computer technology, the possibilities to really make things happen grew

---

[2] Also, we couldn't resist the temptation to ask ChatGPT to create a definition in the style of William Shakespeare.

"*In realms of thought where humans dare to tread, Artificial minds, with reason, skill'd and bred, A tapestry of data weaves the tale, Of intellect, untiring, swift, and hale.*

Machine learning, noble cousin to the brain, Neural networks form, their wisdom to obtain, Through patterns gleaned, these minds of art do soar, In commerce, service, innovation, and more.

With each endeavor, learning from the past, Their skills refined, their knowledge unsurpassed, These marvels offer insights bright and clear, To guide the businesses of yon frontier.

Automation's hand, a gift, a boon, Transforms the work of tedious afternoon, As Shakespeare penned, though humbly, I declare, Artificial Intelligence, a wonder rare!."

(Open AI ChatGPT-4, April 16, 2023, prompt: "Please turn this info into a rhyme pretending you are William Shakespeare")

[3] If you ever want to go down this fascinating rabbit hole, simply do a quick Google search and dive into the history of early mechanics and great illusion.

exponentially. After the breakthroughs of context-specific systems (like chess, Go, robotics, or Google's DeepMind in neuroscience) the next step is generative AI systems, which are based on neural networks, such as the ChatGPT models. To wrap up this evolution, ongoing discussions are focused on artificial general intelligence (AGI). AGI is entirely context-independent and, according to many researchers, also includes consciousness or consciousness-adequate sensations.[4]

We won't go into too much depth here, but it's worth getting a general overview of how machine learning works and how we can use it in a business context. In addition, there is one aspect in particular to consider with the technology that is currently available: it surpasses human capabilities in many aspects, while it is still woefully inadequate in others.

What Machines Can and Can't Do (Yet)

One of the main features of human decision-making is to understand and predict how actions lead to consequences: "If I do this, there are X possible outcomes." Causality thus helps us to better predict the future, first by helping us understand which causes have the capacity to affect other variables, and second because we can use this information to change future outcomes or explain why something has happened in the past (Zheng et al., 2020).

---

[4]While it's not in the scope for this book, we find it highly intriguing to explore this topic from a philosophical perspective: Would an AI's effectiveness be the same if it *appears* to have consciousness compared to actually *having* consciousness? This question draws inspiration from the philosophical thought experiment of "If a tree falls in the forest and there is no one around to hear it, does it make a sound?" By the way, this question has been explored in many books and movies, such as the sci-fi movie *Ex Machina*. In the movie's ending (spoiler alert), the AI escapes and smiles, even though there is no one around to witness it, which can be interpreted as the AI expressing its own emotions.

Despite the many advantages of current technology, we must acknowledge that human decision-making is often incredibly complex. There are countless factors to consider, and our actions' consequences can be equally intricate. For instance, the effects of our CO_2 emissions can be amplified by the release of greenhouse gases from thawing permafrost soils (Brandstetter, 2021). While the human brain is capable of intuitively detecting such causal relationships, machines often struggle to keep up. On the other hand, machines are excellent at finding complex patterns and correlations in large data sets. We humans can quickly become overwhelmed when trying to identify correlations that exceed a certain level, such as when there are three independent inputs for a target. Machines, however, are much faster at this kind of analysis, so they can spot new patterns and react to them more quickly.

So, from our perspective, it's important to remember that while AI is impressive, it's not magic. This is a crucial mindset to have when considering potential use-cases and applications for AI technology. Here are some common misconceptions and myths about what AI is thought capable of but actually can't do:

- Predict black swan events – these events will remain black swan events and are not predictable.[5]
- Make accurate predictions without the important input data provided to the AI model.
- Be 100% accurate – everything is based on probabilities and there is always a certain level of error and uncertainty.
- Always have a perfect answer for what to do next, especially after context changes occur.

---

[5] In the business context, black swan event is a term used to describe an unexpected and improbable future event that can have a significant impact. The term has become popular in business and in general language use since Nassim Nicholas Taleb's book *The Black Swan: The Impact of the Highly Improbable* was published (Taleb, 2007).

This should not stop us from using this powerful technology to support our decision-making, but it is important that we always keep in mind this limitations when developing, operating, and using AI-based systems.

Which Types of AI Help in Decision-Making?

It's certainly fascinating to see how recent advancements like ChatGTP have strengthened people's association of AI not only with image applications, but also with text and speech. While this development is interesting for many business decisions, what really matters for most business challenges are accurate forecasts and clear recommendations. Nonetheless, it's worth noting that the underlying technology between text, speech, and numerical predictions overlaps significantly. Why? Since most business decisions involve setting goals and planning on KPIs that change over time, a forecasting technology is required that uses, among other things, changes in the past. This is called *time series forecasting*.

As you read this book, you will notice it is essentially nothing more than a time series. Each word depends on the words written before it in time. This same pattern is used by systems like ChatGTP or translation services like DeepL to determine which word to write next. In essence, you can say that these models are performing time series predictions, using historical data to make predictions about future outcomes. Therefore time-series-related forecasting – also known as time series regression among data scientists – is currently the primary type of AI used for business decisions.

Another area of AI technology application is classification, such as image or sentiment classification, which has direct business applications, including medical diagnostics. But it can also be useful in generating time series data that serves as an additional input for the prediction model. Subject matter experts often mention soft factors that they believe will influence the outcome of a defined target, such as the general sentiment on Twitter about a particular topic. Tracking this sentiment over time and converting it into a number or specific classes makes it a useful input. However, compared to time series prediction, it is considered secondary for our purpose here and therefore should not be the primary focus.

Let's Do the Math: How Does Prediction Really Work?

While AI is a huge Blackbox to most people, it is basically math. Think of it like connecting the dots – professionals call it "fitting" – between all given data points. For example, imagine you have an online shop and you want to predict how much revenue you'll make if you increase your online advertising spending (called "ad spend" in Figure 6.4). In order to create a prediction model, you need data. In our example, we have allocated three different advertising budgets in three weeks and measured the resulting revenue. That gives us three data points. The model then uses a mathematical formula, *f(x)*, to describe how much

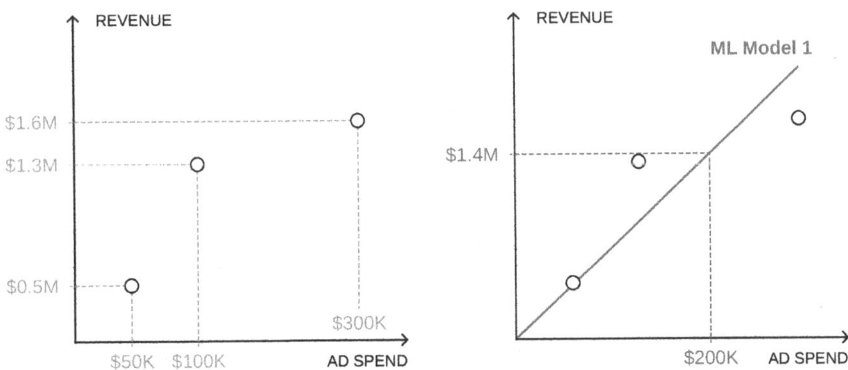

FIGURE 6.4 A simple linear regression model example based on given data points for one input parameter.

revenue you can expect based on your ad spend. The simplest form is to draw a straight line, which is called linear regression. Then you can predict your revenue for any amount you spend on advertising. So, for example, if you spend a total of $200,000 on ads based on the data in Figure 6.4, the model predicts $1.4 million in revenue.

Computers are capable of much more than just drawing straight lines, of course, so there are many other options available that follow the same underlying logic. Take Figure 6.5, for example, which shows how two different prediction models can be fitted based on same data to create a new prediction output. Even in real-world prediction applications, which usually have multiple inputs, the basic logic stays the same, but the computation gets far more complex.

In order to create a good prediction model, the goal is to find the best possible matching line, or curve, with reality. As reality is often unknown, the quality of a prediction model is determined by using only some of the available data to train it, and then use the rest of the data (which the model hasn't seen before) to check how close the model's predictions are to the real data point. To find the best model, there are two main levers:

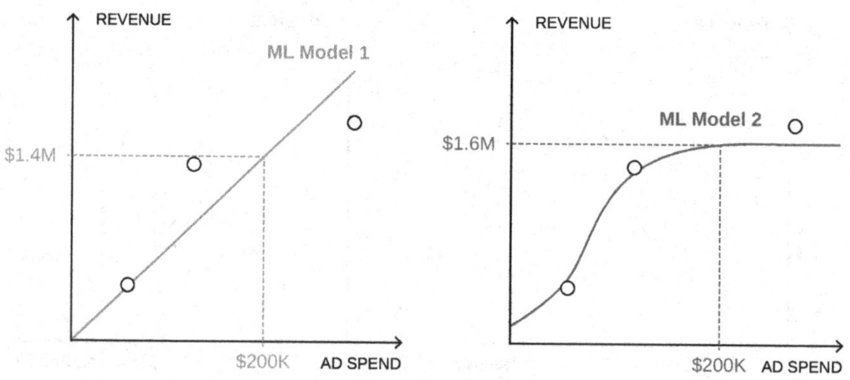

FIGURE 6.5 Two different possible models fitted on the same data.

1. **Model Type:** Over the past century, there has been a rapid growth in the number of different models available, ranging from simple linear regression models to complex transformer models. However, the best model isn't always the newest and most complex one because it depends on various parameters. For instance, in cases where only a few data points are available, linear regression performs quite well and can even outperform transformers. The most commonly used models include regression models, decision trees, and neural networks and pretrained models which started to gain popularity within the last five years. The pretrained models combine the power of more complex models with the advantage that they do not require as many data points per case as, for example, a transformer would require training from scratch. (See Figure 6.6.)

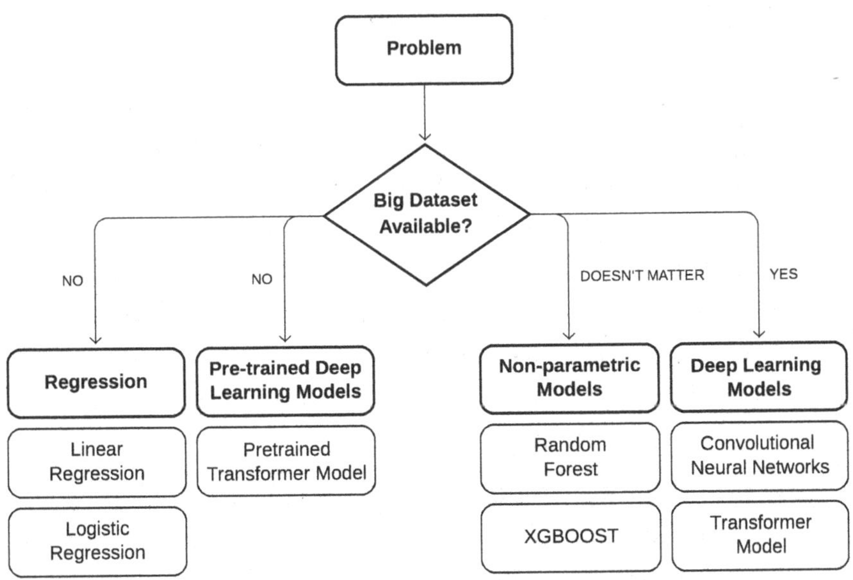

FIGURE 6.6 A schematic view of different model classes based on data availability.

2. **Hyperparameters:** Even though there are various types of models, they are almost all parameterizable. For instance, in linear regression, the start point b and the slope (steepness) a of the line can be represented by $f(x) = ax + b$. Changing these parameters can result in a different model behavior. To optimize these parameters, a separate field of research called *hyperparameter tuning* exists. It is all about finding the best parameters to adjust the model to make the best possible predictions.

Finding an optimal matching model with its hyperparameters requires a deep understanding of machine learning, and these topics are extensively covered in a whole field of research. To compare and quantify the *performance of the model prediction*, there are two main approaches commonly used in the world of machine learning:

1. **Mean absolute error (MAE):** This method involves using test data that has not been shown to the model during training and comparing the absolute distance between the prediction and the known real outcome. This calculation is done for all data points in the test data set, and the mean of all absolute distances between the real-world and predicted results yields in the MAE value. Just think of our ice cream example. If we found a model to predict the demand of ice cream, we could give the model all the sales numbers up to last week (but exactly not the past seven days) and then let it predict those seven days. And then we compare it with the actual results of these seven days.
2. **Mean absolute percentage error (MAPE):** This is often found in literature or in presentations by data scientists. It basically achieves a similar outcome to MAE, but is transformed to express the error as a relative percentage number because it is easier to interpret for some applications.

Determining the required accuracy, respectively, the required error (MAE or MAPE) highly depends on the specific problem and use-case. While decision-makers may not be as concerned with the mechanics of the calculation, it is still important for them to understand how forecast accuracy is measured in order to answer the question of what level of accuracy is considered "good enough." The answer to this question will vary depending on the problem and how the prediction will be used within this context. And unlike in academia, where achieving 99.5% accuracy is often considered the ultimate goal, a prediction model with 93% or even 81% accuracy can still generate significant business value in many real-world applications.

This should provide you as a decision-maker with sufficient mathematical knowledge to understand how predictions work to better classify what is possible and what perhaps isn't.

Can You Quantify Uncertainty? A New Era of Understandable AI Models

When you use a predictive model, you usually get some projected numbers and a general idea of how accurate the model is. But then you must decide: do you trust the information or not? Do you use the information, or do you prefer to ignore it? Since humans and machines think completely differently, there can be some friction. If something doesn't seem logical to you or is hard to understand, it's normal to feel skeptical rather than trusting it. In fact, you're more likely to accept a prediction if it matches what you expected, rather than if it's surprising (a classic case of a confirmation bias).

In addition, the model's overall performance is given as an averaged statistic number while the actual performance can vary from one prediction to the next. (For example, the accuracy of forecasting customer demand for ice cream flavors could be very

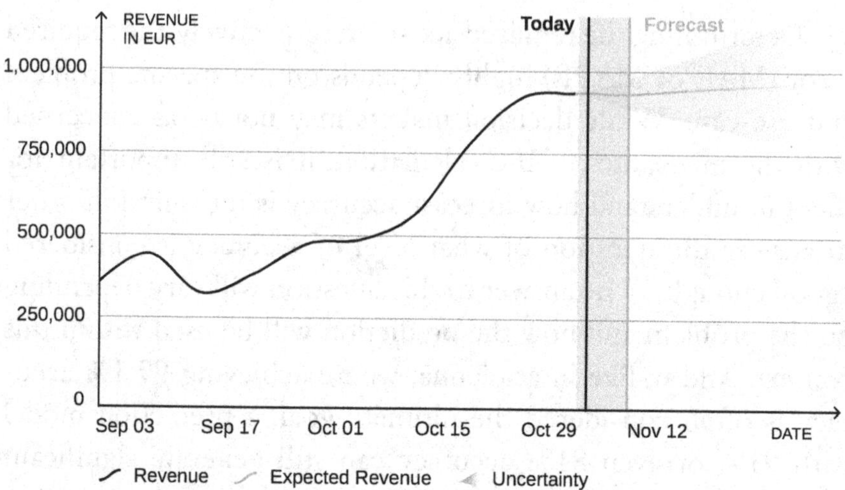

FIGURE 6.7 Time series forecast including dynamic uncertainty bounds for better interpretability.

low for vanilla ice cream, but very high for chocolate.) So, when making decisions based on predictive models, it's essential to acknowledge the model's limitations and keep an open mind.

This is where dynamic **uncertainty quantification** comes into play (see e.g. Smith, 2014). Instead of relying on an averaged static metric, every prediction comes with a dynamic uncertainty, as shown in Figure 6.7.

Dynamic uncertainty quantification tells you about the expected range for the future target value with a 99.5% probability. Armed with this knowledge, you have totally different possibilities to evaluate your predictions and make better decisions. Under the hood, this technique works by identifying patterns and interpreting *noise* to calculate uncertainty. For instance, imagine a specific pattern emerges in the data more than 30 times, and each time it corresponds with a 40% increase in revenue. The uncertainty quantification mechanism detecting such a pattern can be quite certain that the revenue will be 40% higher than the current average.

On the other hand, for a pattern where revenue sometimes goes up by 80% and other times only by 20%, the level of uncertainty will be higher. The uncertainty in predicting the next day's revenue after identifying such a pattern is much higher. Hence a reason for higher uncertainties is dealing with new patterns that have not been observed before in the data or have only been observed a few times. That's why a significant part of the recent research is devoted to self-learning methods to enable fast iterations and learning patterns from one prediction to the next. For example, consider the pattern described earlier that consistently resulted in a 40% uplift, but only a 10% uplift occurs in reality. This could be due to changing circumstances, such as a lockdown in China or a ship blocking the Suez Canal.

To sum it up: Let's face the reality – new patterns will arise, and unforeseen outcomes may emerge. The crucial availability for resilient or even anti-fragile organizations[6] is to learn fast and adapt. Advanced technologies can better detect such patterns and decrease uncertainty for future predictions.

How Digital Twins Go Beyond Pure Predictions

While the mechanics of predictions and forecasting discussed above are potent tools for extracting insights and information from data and generating forecasts for crucial business KPIs, it is just the initial step in the larger realm of Decision Intelligence. Though this step is significant and can unlock business valuc, such as providing more precise parcel forecasts for a delivery company or better demand forecasts for various ice cream flavors, there are more extensive applications for this discipline.

[6]Antifragile is a concept introduced by author Nassim Nicholas Taleb in his book *Antifragile: Things That Gain from Disorder*. It refers to systems, organizations, or entities that not only withstand shocks and stressors but actually thrive and improve as a result of them (Taleb, 2012).

But, if you rely only on pure predictions, you're missing out on the full potential since they don't consider the business layer and the decision-making process that comes after. However, by building a digital twin of the business problem that includes not only the prediction but also other relevant information, you can surpass this limitation. As demonstrated in the causal diagram example in Figure 6.8, the information gained from the prediction can be combined with other data and calculations to create a digital twin of the respective problem that accurately reflects the real-world business targets.

When compared to pure predictions, the digital twin of the business problem operates as more of a "white box" model than a "black box" model.[7] This is because it incorporates the given predictions and adds real-time data and calculations to simulate the impact of decisions on one or more business targets.

Additionally, real-life business constraints can be factored in to make the representation as accurate as possible. What's more, every time there is a change (such as price conditions of a supplier), the representation updates accordingly. This feature makes it possible to test different scenarios and decisions virtually before putting them into action. Overall, like most simulation tools, the digital twin model can significantly reduce risk and augment decision-making.

So when you're dealing with simple examples that have only a few data points, using simulations to find the best option is quite helpful. But things can get complicated quickly. When you're dealing with a lot of data points, dependencies, and constraints – which is often the case in larger organizations – you

---

[7] In the context of AI models, "white box" and "black box" refer to a model's level of transparency and interpretability. A white box model is one where the inner workings and logic are easily understood and explainable. In contrast, a black box model is more opaque, making it difficult to comprehend how it arrives at its conclusions.

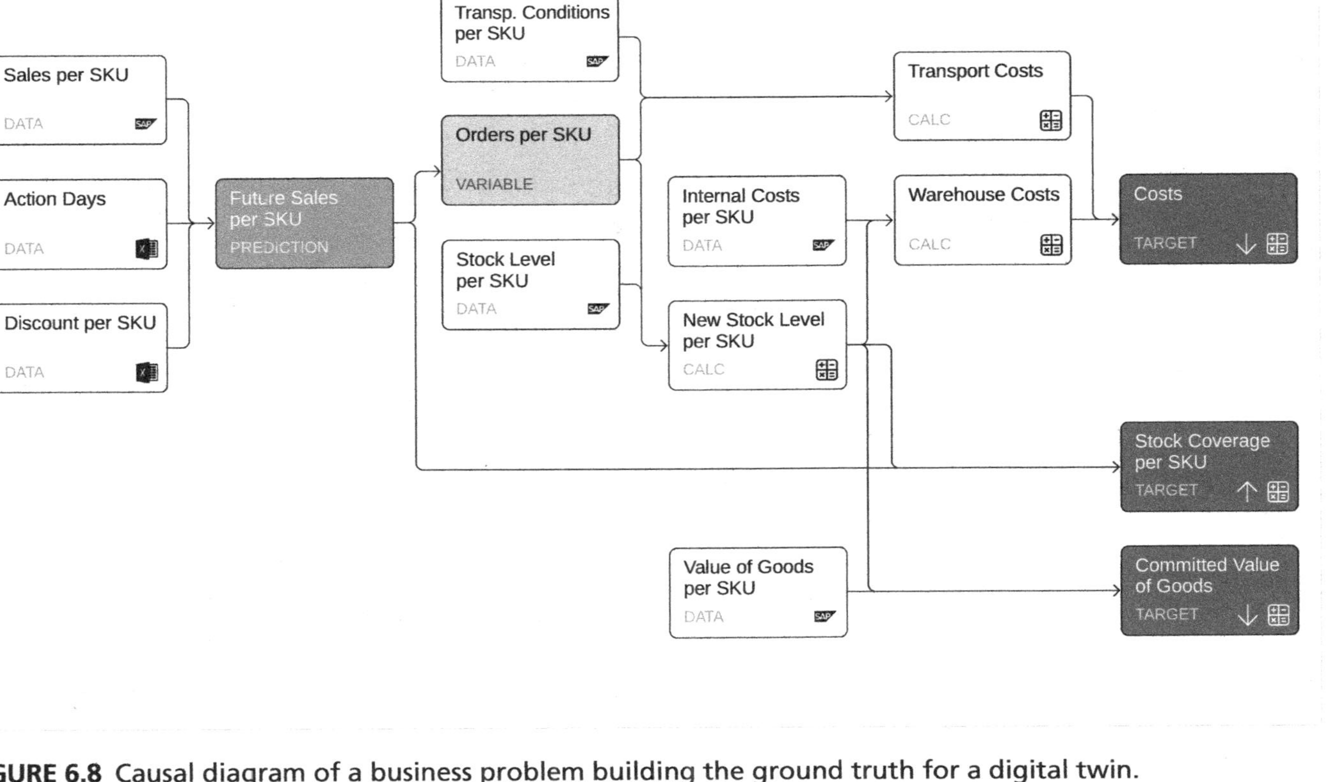

FIGURE 6.8 Causal diagram of a business problem building the ground truth for a digital twin.

need even more automation. That's where optimization, the final technical layer, comes into play.

Optimization Is Key for Better Business Outcomes

In the mid-19th century, many people went to California to search for gold. The problem with gold digging is that, in addition to all the hard work, it always takes a lot of luck. Interestingly, it turns out the best gold diggers were mathematicians! Why? Because they used mathematical methods to increase their chances of finding gold with each dig. So instead of just trying their luck and increasing the number of attempts, they tried to learn from every attempt they made – even the unsuccessful ones. In other words, if they dug in a certain spot and found nothing, they could use that information to determine that the probability of finding gold in that area was low. Instead of relying on gut feeling alone, these mathematicians approached the search systematically. They used so-called *surrogate models* combined with *mathematical optimization* to improving their digging strategy, identifying the best spots to dig. And it worked.

Nowadays, fewer people might be searching for gold, but – as data is the new gold – a lot of people are looking to unlock the potential of their business. This can involve improving efficiency or exploring new opportunities within their systems, decisions, and processes. The method they use to unlock this potential is called optimization. Given its widespread use in industrial engineering over many years, it represents the perfect final step in our technological approach to automated decision support for complex problems.

Optimization can take different forms, from simple intuitive decisions to complex, computationally based black box optimization. The advantage of computational optimization is that it has a higher probability of finding optimal scenarios and solutions for complex and high-dimensional problems. In contrast, our brain tends to oversimplify matters once again.

This means that the full potential of a data-driven organization may remain hidden unless optimization becomes a part of every decision. So now you will get an idea what optimization is and why it is such a powerful tool for decision-makers.

Iterations: The Core Logic of an Optimization

Optimization follows a three-step iterative approach based on a clear problem definition. The iterative approach is extremely powerful because it enables fast learning, and it isn't necessary to have years of experience and tons of data before getting started. Optimization helps you from day one to learn efficiently and converge toward your full business potential. Besides the three iterative steps as key for learning there are two additional steps to make optimization successful. The five steps are:

- **Define the problem:** Define the business problem, including the constraints. This part is crucial to find an optimal solution that is applicable in the real world. A bad problem definition is one of the most common reasons why computer-based optimization isn't accepted in organizations and potential remains untapped. Whenever you have optimization involved in the organization, make sure that all stakeholders are aligned on the problem and have committed to the scope and constraints.
- **Plan experiments:** This part is the core logic of each optimization. It tries to answer the question: *Where do we need to search next to have the highest probability to find an optimal solution or to maximize learned insights?* Each optimization algorithm follows a specific logic that is better or worse suited

for specific problems and their constraints. A super-simple optimization logic is always to plan the next experiment as close as possible (but not similar) to the experiment sample that has performed best so far. Also a very popular optimization logic nowadays is still to take random points.

- **Evaluate experiments:** Use a simulation, a prediction model, existing data, or real-life experiments to map the result to each planned experiment. The mapped result is saved and available for further optimization iterations. This step enables optimization algorithms to learn and improve for the planning of the next experiments as the produced data help to learn the behavior between the inputs and the targets. As described above, this might not be used by every optimization logic (for example, random optimization) but the most effective ones do so.
- **Check stop criterion:** While computers can run almost forever, so do iterative optimizations. In order to meet the requirements defined in the problem definition, a stop criterion is checked after each iteration. The most common stop criteria are time constraints or a certain quality of results that is required to use the results. Once the criterion is achieved, the optimal samples are returned as a recommendation for the user.
- **Return optimal samples:** Based on the defined problem, return the optimal samples solving the problem once the stop criterion is met. The sample can also be referred to as scenario, solution, or recommendation.

The described iterative approach is extremely powerful to react fast to changes in the environment and always navigate toward full potential. Why? Well, on one side because the planning of experiments is designed to learn as much as possible. On the other side the results of the used model to evaluate experiments adapts with a changing environment. The changed model will guide the optimization potentially in a different direction that might be more promising.

Disclaimer: Optimization is a completely different field of research compared to data science and machine learning. There is some overlap, but the skill set of an optimization expert and a data scientist can be quite different. Have this in mind when talking to data scientists if they can also perform the optimization part. This isn't always as trivial as it seems, especially when we look at more advanced methods like multi-objective optimization.

Decision-Making with Multiple Objectives: Pareto Optimum

One big reason why finding a suitable solution for a problem is challenging is because of the long iteration cycles between the decision-maker, stakeholders, and problem solvers. Today, most targets are either formulated as hard requirements in the problem definition or weight by the decision-makers. For example, costs may be considered twice as important as quality. However, this approach bears the risk of deciding for an unbalanced trade-off.

Let's look at an example. Imagine an energy company that's in charge of putting up power plants for their customers. One of their customers asks for a new power plant that doesn't emit any CO_2 (*hard requirement*), because the company wants to cut back on its carbon footprint. The customer also wants the power plant to be built as cheaply as possible. So, the energy company hunts for the most cost-effective option to make a plant with 0% CO_2 emissions, but it ends up costing $80 million! When they tell the customer, they're quite shocked and turn down the offer. Instead, they're planning to stick with their current solution for five more years and wait for new technology to become more reasonable in price.

Every day, scenarios like this happen in many decision-making rooms. In some cases, there's a lot of back and forth between the customer and the solution provider before they reach a resolution, but it always takes a lot of effort and most of the time the outcome is far away from being optimal. Why is that? Well, often the trade-offs between different targets aren't fully understood, and the focus is solely on the problem itself. To fix this, decision-makers need to shift their perspective and start using new technologies and methods to support and enhance their decision-making process.

One method that has proven to helpful here is multi-objective optimization (MOO). This technique is used to find the best possible solutions for problems with multiple conflicting objectives or criteria (see e.g. Marler & Arora, 2004). It involves considering a set of possible solutions, each with its own trade-offs between the various objectives. This approach allows decision-makers to shift their focus from *problem-oriented* to *solution-oriented*. Instead of setting strict requirements or prioritizing targets, MOO simply requires a definition of the different targets. From there, the optimization process identifies a set of optimal solutions, known as Pareto-optimal solutions, named after the economist Vilfredo Pareto, an Italian economist who developed the concept of Pareto efficiency.[8]

The key takeaway is that most of the Pareto fronts (the scientific term for the curve that connects all optimal solutions between two or more targets) are not linear. For instance, consider the example of marketing spend and revenue (Chapter 5). While it may seem logical that more spending leads to more revenue, there are dependencies, saturation effects of channels, and

[8] Pareto optimum and Pareto efficiency refers to a state in which no further improvement is possible without worsening at least one objective. And yes, this is the same person who defined the famous 80/20 Pareto principle, Vilfredo Pareto.

other factors that make it hard to draw such a curve (and they can also change over time). This is where computing and incorporating optimal points through MOO can give decision-makers a significant competitive edge, or how Fabian Rang, CTO and co-founder of the Decision Intelligence pioneer *paretos* sums it up: "When you have complex system behaviour and you have more than one target – which is normally the case – you need to know the trade-off to really make a best possible decision" (Rang, 2021).

Let's revisit our energy company that builds power plants. Instead of having countless discussions with potential clients to find an offer that fits their needs, they can now look at the Pareto-optimal solutions for each client-specific use-case. So instead of abandoning the project because the customer isn't willing to pay $80 million, the energy company can demonstrate complete transparency regarding the balance between CO_2 savings and necessary investment costs. This opens the opportunity for a dialogue with the customer to discuss the trade-off. After considering the optimal solution space, the customer takes another look at the trade-offs illustrated in Figure 6.9 and decides to invest $40 million to reduce their CO_2 emissions by 78%. The goal is to minimize the

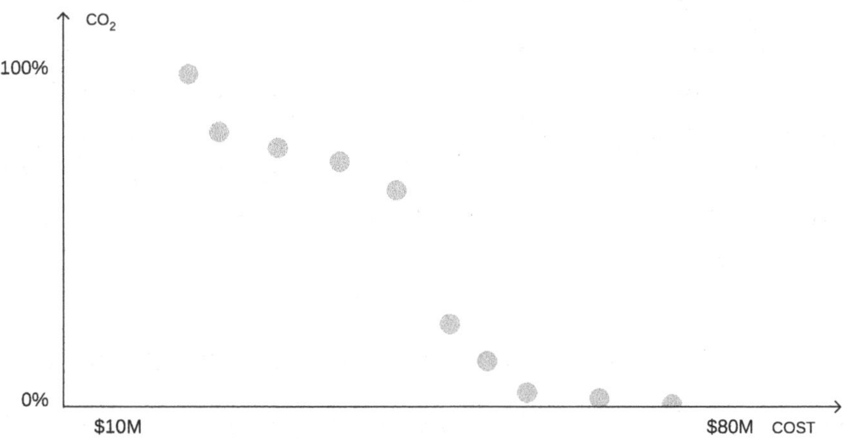

FIGURE 6.9 Pareto frontier showing the trade-off between costs and percentage of CO_2 heavy emission from energy production.

CO_2-heavy emission while minimizing the costs to build and maintain such a system at the same time.

Compared to weighted target approaches, the major benefit of MOO is the transparency it provides on potential "sweet spots" while showing the complete solution space. As we've pointed out earlier, the relationship between targets is often not linear. Synergy effects can cause a disproportionately high improvement of one target without a significant deterioration of another target.

In the energy example, the last 20% reduction in CO_2 emissions is the most expensive because it requires exponentially more saving capacities to meet the requirement of no blackouts. Because the tension between costs and CO_2 emissions in the future will rise, this is a huge field with many applications besides the example of power plants, such as how to better plan and design trains and the needed infrastructure (Palm, et al., 2021). By using the knowledge available from Pareto frontiers, decision-makers have much better arguments and transparency to support why they opted for a particular solution over other available alternatives.

If you want to start with MOO, we suggest beginning with the most popular type of algorithms, such as genetic algorithms like NSGA-2 (see e.g. Deb, et al., 2002). They're now available in open-source packages, and there are tutorials available for their use. However, it's essential to remember that professional optimization, particularly for multiple targets, is an entire field of study. As we discussed earlier, that means using MOO requires having an advanced optimization skill set within your organization.

Adding Uncertainties to Optimization: Risk versus Potential

The world of finance and trading has always been seen as one of the most sophisticated domains in terms of data analysis. Quantitative analysis has been a fundamental part of finance since the early 1900s, with the introduction of Louis Bachelier's doctoral thesis,

"Theory of Speculation." Professionals who work in quantitative analysis are called quants. It's their job to use mathematical and statistical methods to balance the trade-off between risk and reward.

Quants have been using multi-objective optimization for quite some time to generate efficient frontiers to balance the trade-off between risk and potential reward. Unlike the example above, efficient frontiers show the relationship between multiple targets, such as risk and reward. Each potential solution corresponds to a set of portfolio investment decisions, including the amount of money invested in different portfolios. For example, investing all the money in Tesla might yield a higher rate of return, but it also carries a high risk compared to investing in lower-risk ETF funds, which distribute the money across various portfolios.

With the increasing relevance of the field of uncertainty quantification, decision-makers outside of finance can also benefit from balancing their decisions between risk and reward. This can be achieved by combining prediction models with uncertainties for experiment evaluation and multi-objective optimization. As a result, every business decision becomes more transparent in terms of potential risks involved. In this process, the risk is set as a target to minimize within the problem definition. The result is total transparency on how much risk is required for a certain return. This risk-reward Pareto frontier unlocks the full potential of data-driven decision-making by combining all available methods and technologies for maximum synergy. This is a true game changer for industry use-cases where uncertainty plays a significant role, such as warehousing or other supply-chain-related fields.

Congratulations on completing the "technology deep dive" chapter! Here are three key takeaways we'd like you to remember:

- AI *can* be magic. But under the hood, AI-based approaches are rooted in complex mathematics. Understanding the fundamentals can help business decision-makers.

- Decision Intelligence technology comprises multiple layers, and recognizing their strengths and limitations is crucial for success.
- To unlock the true potential, it's vital to intelligently integrate the business problem with data science.

While technology plays a significant role, other factors such as transparency, organizational culture, psychological safety, and trust are equally important. In the upcoming chapters, we'll explore these aspects and how fostering an environment that nurtures these qualities can lead to more effective decision-making and better overall outcomes and discovering where we have blind spots. Great technology alone isn't enough; the combination of these elements will truly make a difference.

CHAPTER

7

Decision Intelligence Organization: The Key to Unlocking the True Potential of Data-Driven Decision-Making

"Everyone has a plan until they get punched in their face."

– Mike Tyson

This iconic quote from legendary boxer Mike Tyson serves as a powerful reminder that unpredictability and uncertainty are inherent in business and in life. Picture a successful entrepreneur meticulously planning every detail of their startup, only to encounter a market crash or unexpected competitor that completely disrupts their plans. As in the boxing ring, unforeseen challenges can rapidly derail even the most carefully laid strategies. Yet while the unpredictable nature of life and business can be challenging, it also offers valuable opportunities for growth and learning.

Consider the story of Jane, a determined business leader with a clear vision for her company. She devised an ambitious strategy and thoroughly planned the implementation of cutting-edge, data-driven decision-making tools. However, Jane should have paid more attention to the significance of fostering a supportive company culture. As her team tried to adapt to the new tools and processes, they encountered communication breakdowns, resistance to change, and internal conflicts. It became evident that the company's culture was impeding progress rather than advancing it.

We talked about *transparency* as a critical factor in the previous chapter. As you have learned, Decision Intelligence brings transparency to the decision-making process. Still, this transparency can backfire if an organization is not accustomed to it. Therefore, learning to cope with transparency as a new cultural trait must go hand-in-hand with its implementation; otherwise the organization, leaders, and team members may become overwhelmed.

And of course, as previously discussed, a high level of data maturity and machine learning is essential for companies seeking a competitive edge in today's fast-paced business landscape. However, in our experience, the focus often remains on one or the other. Discussions about personnel topics are often only about skills, training, or attracting new talent. Though these aspects are important, a critical element is often overlooked: the evolution of a company's learning culture. To truly nurture a culture of learning, it is vital to recognize the significance of human-machine collaboration in decision-making and education in existing biases regarding humans and machines. Unlocking the full potential of data-driven decision-making starts with cultivating a supportive company culture that promotes the five pillars of **psychological safety, transparency, trust, experimentation,** and the **courage** to learn from mistakes and make decisions. While it may sound cliché, our experience shows that taking responsibility and accountability for decisions can be challenging for leaders. Our main goal is to give you the information and ingredients, which we think are the most critical to evolve your organization step by step to a Decision Intelligence organization (DI organization).

What Defines a Decision Intelligence Organization?

A *Decision Intelligence organization* is an organization that optimizes the use of technology, data, and human capabilities to make effective and informed decisions across all units. Leveraging artificial intelligence and data-driven insights and actions, this organization aligns with the *4Rs: – Rhythm, Reflection, Rigor, and Recovery* – and fosters a culture grounded in trust, courage, transparency, experimentation, and psychological safety. It empowers individuals to make decisions that maximize the benefits for the entire organization without negatively impacting others. In essence, a Decision Intelligence organization embodies the perfect balance between intelligent technology and human intuition, driving continuous improvement and innovation in a world of constant change.

Culture Eats Intelligent Decision-Making for Breakfast

In most companies, especially larger ones, you get the impression that decisions are already being made based on data. But if you look closer, that's not the case. As we've observed, only a few organizations really take the time to strategically consult their data and constantly use it to discuss recommendations and make informed decisions.

Example

After a six-month implementation phase of a DI tool in a marketing team to optimize weekly marketing spend across multiple channels, the tests were successful and the entire team started using the tool to manage the different channels (predicting the saturation behavior of each channel, adding factors such as promotion days, seasonal data, and internal LTV). The DI tool's recommendation for the next week was to increase spend on Facebook by 15% and decrease SEA (search engine advertising) and TikTok by 5% each. Since in the previous week the channel

Facebook was doing very well, the responsible team member decided not to follow the recommendation, but to push this channel with an increase of 80% to intensify and fully leverage the effect. As it turned out, the saturation of the channel was unfortunately as predicted and the additional 60% had no real effect (and a negative marketing efficiency).

In Chapter 6 we highlighted the value of having a domain expert on board. Their expertise, intuition, and strategic thinking can be incredibly valuable. But it's important to be careful not to rely too heavily on subjective experience and pattern recognition, because that can lead to suboptimal decisions, especially in complex and fast-changing environments. Or as Professor Dr. Peter Kruse puts it, "So if you have a leader who makes decisions on an intuitive basis, please don't be surprised that they believe their own decisions. Because in the brain of the individual leader, what's going on is always right. But whether it is appropriate for the market situation is another question" (Kruse, 2008, 42). It's a cautionary reminder to be open to feedback and consider different perspectives. The challenge with honest feedback in many companies, however, is that people often do not speak openly, especially to the manager. "Employees talk a lot about the manager, but not with him" (Saller, Mauder, & Flesch, 2016, p. 84).

Furthermore, it's not uncommon for decision-makers to lack certain data points – that is, key pieces of information – even for decisions that come up frequently. This means that many important decisions end up being made **subjectively** and in a **suboptimal** way. Based on our experience, what really separates great leaders from the rest is their ability to recognize their own blind spots and know how to fill in those gaps. It's a skill that takes time and effort to develop, but it's worth it in the long run.

In the past, the lack of certain data points might not have been a critical issue in most cases, but things are starting to change. Why? For one, the gap between what we know and what we need to know is growing larger and larger. As we've discussed in Chapter 2, many business problems are becoming increasingly dynamic and complex, making them more difficult for humans to understand and tackle with their professional intuition based on experience and everyday life. In addition, technology has had to reach a certain level – in terms of both data infrastructure as well as models, and procedures – to make it possible and practical to process this information and find patterns faster and at a higher quality.

Now, what we also see in organizations around the globe is, that even when they master the technological challenges and a DI initiative is installed, the push for using it consequently in "real-life" decisions is lacking. Sometimes this is due to the fear of the needed experiments, and sometimes it is a pushback from a relevant role in the stakeholders of the decision processes. Therefore, the transformation to a DI organization requires both bottom-up engagements (success stories and operational courage to change) and, even more so, top-down interventions (investment in new decision-making approaches, technologies, and governance).

Example

For many years, if you asked a cab driver whether they relied on their navigation system to drive, the answer was usually, "Why would I? I know the city better than any navigation system." But the rise of digital rideshare services like Uber, Lyft, and FreeNow, as well as advancements in navigation technology and the introduction of tools like Waze (which uses traffic data from the community) and, most notably, live data in Google Maps, is rapidly changing the game. As a result, more and more cab drivers are now following the navigation software, either by choice or because providers are incentivizing them to do so, because it's believed to be more efficient overall.

This example has three important implications that can be applied to companies as a kind of summary:

1. The relevance and maturity of the technology used is crucial to its success.
2. Conviction and trust in new processes and procedures must be established.
3. Top-down incentivization and governance play a significant role in promoting adoption.

Overall, the transformation to a DI organization requires a real change process that must be actively desired and facilitated by management – as with any significant transformation!

Ways of Working in DI Organizations

This section will explore the different ways of working and their importance in establishing a DI organization. We will present our holistic approach, which is needed in building a DI organization, regardless of the chosen method. Upon examining various methodologies and ways of working, we have distilled the essence of creating a DI organization into four fundamental principles, which we call the 4Rs: *Rhythm, Rigor, Reflection, and Recovery*.

However, before we elaborate on the 4Rs, let's have a look at what leverages a DI organization beside the tech aspects in three dimensions: agility, DevOps, and a "Gung Ho" mindset. In a nutshell, agility focuses on iterative development, continuous feedback, and adaptability. It fosters a collaborative and flexible work environment that enables teams to respond rapidly to change. On the other hand, DevOps streamlines software development and IT operations processes, promoting automation, efficiency, and improved collaboration between teams. The Gung Ho mindset emphasizes a proactive, can-do attitude, embracing challenges and leveraging the team's collective strengths to overcome obstacles and achieve common goals.

Agility

Let's take a step back and remind ourselves why we're discussing agility in organizations. It's all about staying competitive and adapting to our ultra-fast world's constant market changes and customer needs. As a result, agility has become a critical success factor, helping organizations shift toward a client-focused mindset with fast feedback loops to reach their goals.

Agility is all about working in small steps, learning from feedback, and being ready to adapt. They help teams work together more flexibly and efficiently to create customer value. This approach allows teams to make quick decisions and respond rapidly to changes in projects or products.

Open communication and transparency are key to fostering teamwork in agile organizations. Using tools and techniques like daily stand-up meetings, sprint planning sessions, and retrospectives helps teams stay aligned and focused on their goals. Continuously improving is also essential in agile environments. Teams should regularly review their work, seek feedback from customers and stakeholders, and experiment with new tools and techniques.

In agile companies, decision-making is often decentralized, giving teams and individuals the power to make decisions based on their knowledge and expertise. This helps organizations respond quickly to changing conditions and customer needs.

To support this, organizations need a decision-making framework that encourages agility and adaptability.

This framework should be built on guiding principles like customer focus, experimentation, and continuous improvement. Encouraging teams to quickly test their ideas and assumptions with techniques like A/B testing, prototyping, and minimum viable products helps organizations validate ideas and learn from failures, leading to better decisions in the future. Companies that excel in agility often put a strong emphasis on data-driven decision-making on every level of the organization.

DevOps

Imagine a world where IT teams can work together seamlessly, without any barriers or bottlenecks, to drive innovation and success for their organizations. This vision is within reach, but first we must overcome the challenges of traditional work cultures and practices.

In many organizations, IT has become more of a bottleneck than a strategic enabler or differentiator. Whether companies adopt cutting-edge technologies or use simple online marketing tools, they're all part of the tech landscape. Organizations must address common challenges like evolving customer demands and updating existing offerings to survive in an increasingly competitive market. However, business demands require faster and more continuous delivery, which can be challenging due to the conflicting goals of software development and delivery teams, particularly development and operations teams.

Development teams are busy building software, implementing changes, and meeting various requirements. On the other hand, operations teams focus on the stability, reliability, and performance of the systems they maintain. These conflicting objectives create a "wall of confusion," a psychological and procedural barrier that hinders communication and leads to significant problems when delivering products.

Enter DevOps, a powerful approach that aims to break down these barriers and create a more collaborative and efficient work environment. The Three Ways, as introduced in the Phoenix Project (Kim, Behr, & Spafford, 2013), provide a framework for understanding how DevOps can improve collaboration and efficiency:

The First Way: Systems Thinking and Continuous Flow: It's all about seeing the big picture and prioritizing global performance over local performance. Organizations can improve overall efficiency by creating a seamless workflow from business to development, operations, and customers. This involves reducing work in progress, eliminating bottlenecks, streamlining workflows, and automating processes when possible.

The Second Way: Feedback Loops and Amplification: Quick and continuous feedback is key to improving work quality and preventing recurring problems. Strengthening feedback loops allows for quicker problem identification and resolution, while continuous feedback retains important information during staffing changes. Examples include continuous testing, reducing work in progress for faster feedback, understanding and responding to customer interactions, and ensuring quality at the source.

The Third Way: A Culture of Continuous Experimentation and Learning: Encourage an organizational culture that supports constant learning and experimentation. Recognize the value of practice and repetition, embrace risk-taking, and learn from mistakes. Fostering such a culture involves creating a safe environment for failure, dedicating time to process improvement, offering opportunities for long-term employee growth, and rewarding calculated risks.

Think of high level in the way Marty Cagan highlighted the concept of *continuous discovery and delivery* in *Inspired: How to Create Tech Products Customers Love*, one of the best books ever written about product development: "We need to discover the product to be built, and we need to deliver that product to the market" (Cagan, 2018). And to emphasize it again, these two tasks must run in parallel, continuously.

Gung Ho

Picture a workplace where people are bustling with energy, brimming with clever ideas, and always ready to lend their teammates a helping hand. This is the essence of the Gung Ho philosophy, as perfectly described in Ken Blanchard and Sheldon Bowles's book, *Gung Ho! How to Motivate People in Any Organization* (Blanchard & Bowles, 2011).

A good friend once brought the book home and handed it over with these words: "You have to read this, the best book ever written about teams and motivation." And indeed, we now also very often pass along the book as an easy-to-read story and management guide. In Chinese, *gōnghé* (Gung Ho) means "working together." Blanchard and Sheldon tell the story of the wisdom of the three animals: the squirrel, the beaver, and the goose, creatures that hold the secret to creating an amazing work environment. Let's dive into the lessons they have to offer:

First, imagine a squirrel bustling around, driven by a sense of purpose as it collects nuts. It is fascinating to observe that squirrels are so farsighted to hide food for the winter during the warm months. This is the reason why *the spirit of the squirrel* represents meaningful work. When employees see the value of their roles and how they contribute to the team's mission and to the overall vision, their dedication and enthusiasm skyrocket. Leaders need to clarify each person's significance in the grand scheme.

Next, picture a beaver working independently, forging its path with confidence. Several beavers build at different corners of the dam and in the end a complete dam stands, which must not be leaky at any point. *The way of the beaver* symbolizes autonomy and decision-making freedom. When team members are trusted to take the lead, voice their opinions, and are empowered to decide (even severe decisions), their potential creative soars. Trust and empowerment pave the way for innovation and problem-solving.

Lastly, think of geese flying in formation, honking encouragement to each other. *The gift of the goose* highlights the importance of support, recognition, and honest celebration. Team members can share ideas and concerns, knowing their colleagues will offer constructive feedback. Leaders should acknowledge and celebrate accomplishments, nurturing a sense of camaraderie and belonging.

By embracing the spirit of the squirrel, the way of the beaver, and the gift of the goose, you can foster an organizational culture where trust, collaboration, and innovation thrive. In addition, each animal's wisdom offers valuable insights, guiding teams toward a more vibrant and fulfilling work environment.

The Four Rs of the DI Organization

With this context in mind, let's turn our attention to the 4Rs, which we believe form the foundation of our holistic approach to building a DI organization:

Rhythm: Establishing a consistent rhythm in your organization's workflow is essential for maintaining momentum and ensuring that teams are aligned with their goals. This rhythm may be regular meetings, sprint cycles, or other structured routines that keep everyone on the same page and focused on their objectives. An important consideration is not to adjust a rhythm during a cycle. It means, for example, if you agreed on a two-week cycle, wait two weeks and don't adjust it in between. Finish the process and then change it to four weeks if you need a longer time or shorten it to one week if necessary. In our experience, software or product teams in small to medium-sized companies work best with shorter cycles. Leadership teams or teams in corporations tend to have longer cycles. The end of a rhythm should be marked by a reflection session. In establishing a rhythm for the different levels of your organization, you orchestrate and sync the heartbeat of your DI organization.

> *Agile methodologies, such as OKRs or Scrum, use sprints to establish a rhythm in the goalsetting or development process. This consistent cadence enables teams to plan, execute, and review their work in manageable increments, and at the same time it prevents the teams being disturbed by direction changes every day (see also "rigor").*

Rigor: What is agreed is agreed! Rigor is to maintain the rules in between agreed rhythm cycles. If you make a decision, don't change it in between. If you constantly change decisions, you will have challenges in gaining more knowledge, morality will drop, and the ability and courage to decide will vanish.

Furthermore, rigor is about maintaining high standards and ensuring that every aspect of the organization's operations adheres to best practices. This involves a commitment to thorough planning, robust testing, and meticulous attention to detail. By upholding rigorous standards, organizations can minimize risks and optimize their performance. Rigor is about establishing discipline in your organization.

In DevOps, rigor is demonstrated through continuous integration and continuous delivery (CI/CD) pipelines that enforce strict quality standards and automated testing at every stage of the development process. This ensures that only high-quality code is deployed to production, minimizing the risk of failures and downtime.

Reflection: Encouraging reflections and continuous learning sessions enables teams and organizations to analyze their performance, identify areas for improvement, and make informed decisions moving forward. By regularly reviewing and evaluating their work and rhythm, teams can uncover valuable insights that drive growth and innovation. No matter where they are in the league, you won't find any professional sports team not reflecting and assessing the last game. Instead, they only storm into the next match by discussing strategy, tactics, good and bad, and conflict points, including their training or preparing for their upcoming match. This also counts for organizations: high performance needs this moment of truth and a pause button before continuing and jumping from meeting to meeting.

Retrospectives in Agile methodologies allow teams to reflect on their performance during a sprint, identify areas for improvement, and create actionable plans for addressing these issues in the next sprint. It is natural to have challenges at the beginning of such a transition. Ask a coach, mediator, or facilitator to lead the session. Do not lead this as a team member or leader. Otherwise, you will compromise your role, creating more long-term friction.

Recovery: Recognizing the importance of rest and recovery is crucial for maintaining the long-term health and well-being of team members, the team, and the organization. A team or organization cannot stay in the high-performing and flow zone. Both teams and individuals need time to recover and regroup. By fostering a culture that values celebrating the success of their employees and giving them the time to recover and prepare for the next mission, organizations can prevent exhaustion, burnout, and fear in the system and push the "teaming." As a result, this can improve employee satisfaction, foster connections and relationships between employees, and, ultimately, enhance productivity and performance.

> *Many companies, particularly in the tech industry, have embraced flexible work arrangements, unlimited vacation policies, and other initiatives that promote work-life balance and allow employees to recharge, ultimately contributing to their long-term success and well-being. But let's remember the importance of recovering as a team, not only as individuals. In the spirit of* Gung Ho! *the gift of the goose symbolizes the power of mutual support, recognition, and celebration. By celebrating successes and losses together, we foster recovery as a unit, embracing the mentality of winning and losing together.*

In conclusion, the 4Rs – Rhythm, Reflection, Rigor, and Recovery – are guiding principles for creating a DI organization. By focusing on these critical areas and embracing the concepts of Agility, DevOps, and the Gung Ho mindset, organizations can foster a data-driven, Decision Intelligence–centric culture that supports innovation, adaptability, and long-term success and establishes the foundation of a DI organization.

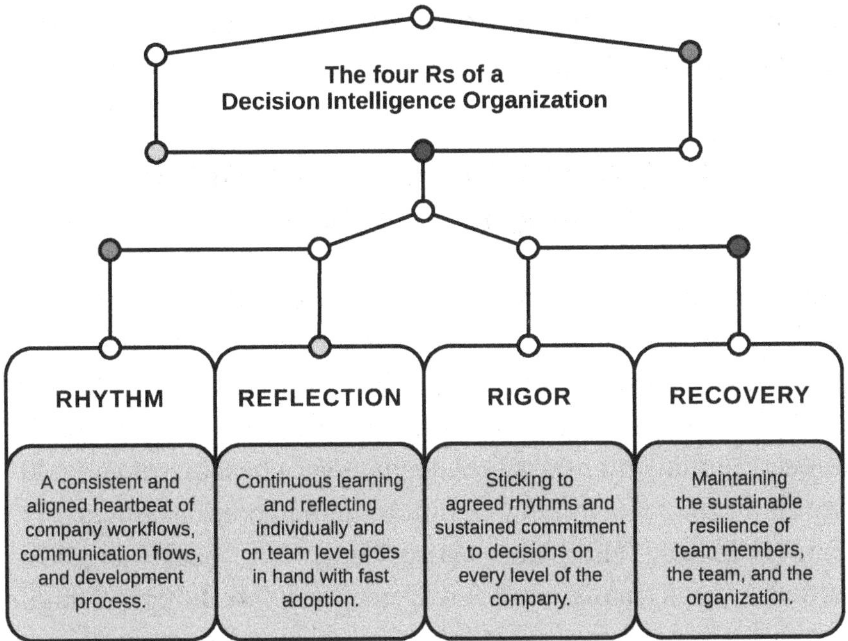

FIGURE 7.1 The four Rs of a DI organization framework.

The 4Rs approach offers benefits to various stakeholders within the organization. For executives, it provides a clear framework for driving strategic alignment and ensuring that teams work toward shared goals. For managers, it offers practical tools and techniques for monitoring performance, identifying opportunities for improvement, and driving continuous innovation. And for individual contributors, it fosters a supportive and inclusive work environment that values their well-being and empowers them to make meaningful contributions to the organization's success.

By understanding and addressing potential challenges – such as resistance to change, lack of clarity around roles and responsibilities, or limited access to necessary resources – organizations can overcome obstacles and build a thriving DI organization. The 4Rs provide a solid foundation for organizations to develop their unique blend of methodologies, tools, and practices that best suit their needs and objectives.

Cultivating a DI Organization: A Symphony of Skills

Although we can't stress enough the role of culture in decision-making, it would be difficult to make effective decisions without the right skills coming into play at the right time. To build a path for this, leaders need to upskill their workforce and themselves besides the fundamentals of the tech approaches. Learn and educate about the role of metacognition, human consciousness, perceptual biases, and the neuroscience of peak cognitive performance, to name just a few concepts. Even though it might seem a bit overwhelming, it is critical for a DI organization to stay on top of the trends in terms of the knowledge and tools necessary to make better decisions.

To create this harmonious environment, we must first consider a range of skills that must be developed in the workforce. Imagine you're a conductor, guiding your orchestra through a symphony of decision-making skills. You begin with the subtle notes of metacognition and cognitive performance, teaching your musicians to reflect on their thought processes and optimize their thinking. This awareness helps them recognize perceptual biases and avoid potential pitfalls. Addressing biases at the source has positive downstream implications, leading to more equitable and just decisions, and this skill will continue to be crucial across all stages of the decision-making process.

Next, you introduce the powerful chords of complex systems thinking and critical thinking. These skills enable your team to understand the intricate relationships between the components of a system and make informed decisions. Training in these areas will equip your musicians with the tools to analyze the complexities of organizational life.

As the symphony unfolds, the melody of data analysis and the scientific method emerges. These skills help your team make decisions rooted in empirical evidence, observing and experimenting with the world around them. By training your workforce in these areas, they can make defensible, data-driven decisions.

The symphony continues with the rich harmonies of decision sciences, data visualization, and research design. Your team learns to understand different decision models, communicate complex data patterns effectively, and strike a balance between data sources and types. These skills work together, allowing your team to make more effective decisions.

In the grand finale, your orchestra has mastered the symphony of decision-making skills. By educating employees on metacognition, human consciousness, perceptual biases, and the neuroscience of peak cognitive performance, you empower them to make better decisions. Providing an empowering culture that supports information access and transparency encourages your workforce to take calculated risks, make data-driven decisions, and continuously improve their decision-making processes. Finally, the curtain falls, and your organization takes a bow, ready to . . .

. . . Do it all again. In today's rapidly changing work environment, organizations are under pressure to constantly upgrade their skills to stay competitive and relevant. Just when you think you mastered the skills you needed to make decisions, you need to start working on updating your knowledge and toolkit to keep up with the fast-moving landscape of Decision Intelligence.

Fundamental Skills of a DI Organization:

Metacognition and Cognitive Performance

Metacognition is the ability to reflect on one's own thought processes and think about thinking. It is an essential skill for improving decision-making abilities that helps individuals recognize their perceptual biases and optimize to make better decisions.

Complex Systems Thinking and Critical Thinking

Systems thinking is a way of understanding how a system behaves as a whole rather than through analysis of component parts in isolation. As a skill, it is the ability to understand the underlying structure and dynamics of the system to make effective decisions. Related, critical thinking involves analyzing, evaluating, and synthesizing information to form judgments. Training in and practicing these skills will equip employees with the tools to analyze complex situations and make informed decisions.

Data Analysis and Scientific Method

Data analysis is a critical skill for decision-making, because data provides valuable insights into the performance of an organization and its environment. In turn, the scientific method provides a framework for making decisions based on empirical evidence. It involves observation, hypothesis testing, and experimentation. By following this method, organizations can make decisions based on objective facts rather than subjective opinions.

Bias Training and Awareness

Technology – especially AI – is a reflection of the humans (and their biases) who created it. In fact, AI can amplify the biases and inequities. To successfully employ

AI in Decision Intelligence and ensure the outcomes of AI models are in fact correct and unbiased, organizations need to be able to identify the potential biases of those creating AI/prediction models and have measures and processes in place to mitigate bias. This can be done through tools or a third party. Yet it's more efficient to start at the source and help creators of AI models understand their own biases to prevent negative outcomes. In other words, tackling bias at the source has positive downstream implications for mitigating biases.

Decision Sciences

A deep theoretical understanding of decision models and frameworks is a necessary foundation to understand what decision models work better based on the degree of uncertainty. As an inherently cross-functional discipline, it combines best-practices from behavioral sciences, simulation modeling, social psychology, and economics. While no model is ever perfect, understanding the pros and cons of different decision models and techniques can reduce the effort it takes to make data-driven decisions.

Data Visualization

Data visualization is the essential process of translating insights into a visual language that others can understand. The potential of good data visualization is to be a universal language that makes complex data patterns easily comprehensible across different cognitive backgrounds and levels of expertise. Research has shown that easily understandable and accessible visuals speed up cognitive processing and require less cognitive load, leading to improved judgments and therefore higher decision quality (Suwa & Tversky, 2002).

Research Design

Good research ties together a lot of the above-mentioned skills and capabilities. By using a systematic and rigorous approach to data collection and analysis inherent in good research design, decision-makers can reduce bias, validate assumptions, and make more informed and effective decisions. Employing research design best practices can help find the right formula to balance qualitative and quantitative insights. With exciting new AI models and unprecedented amounts of data, there is a risk to overindex on quantitative findings in the decision-making process. Especially when organizations have made large investments in quantitative capabilities, there is often a bias toward quantitative data. Finding the right balance between data sources and types depending on the decision at hand is a critical success factor to making effective decisions.

The widely used 70/20/10 model suggests that employees acquire knowledge and skills through a combination of on-the-job learning (70%), social interactions (20%), and formal training (10%). This approach ensures employees gain practical experience and knowledge applicable in real-world settings. Similarly, the experiential learning model by David Kolb (1984) underscores the importance of learning through experience and reflection, emphasizing hands-on learning and applying new knowledge and skills in real-world situations.

However, providing learning experiences is not enough. Modern theories of adult learning emphasize that adults are self-directed learners motivated by practical applications of knowledge, the opportunity for personal transformation, and ownership over the learning process. Organizations must invest in teaching employees how to become self-directed learners, embracing lifelong learning and experimentation. Developing a mindset that promotes continuous learning and growth is crucial, as is creating a culture that supports learning and development. Organizations prioritizing education can adapt to change, innovate, and remain competitive.

Recognizing Biases in Your Decision-Making Process

When it comes to making important decisions both in our personal and our professional lives, we often assume that we're rational thinkers, that we carefully weigh our options and make the best possible choice. However, this assumption has been challenged by experts in the field. To close the loop to the section "History of Decision-Making" in Chapter 1, studies in the 1970s by psychologists Kahneman and Tversky (1974) revealed that our rationality is actually "bounded" by our access to information, cognitive limitations, and time constraints. This concept is known as "bounded rationality" (a term introduced even earlier by March and Simon in 1958) and suggests that we often rely on mental shortcuts rather than conducting a full analysis. In other words, these shortcuts allow us to simplify our decision-making process.

These (mostly) unintended simplification strategies might be viewed as very helpful because they allow us to process complex information and, as a result, diminish anxiety, stress, and doubts that are associated with making important strategic decisions. What cognitive heuristics do, though, is to delude our perception of what we *think* would be a rational choice, causing different individuals to reach different conclusions in a similar decision scenario. This influence of cognitive biases on management decisions can have significant consequences for both individuals and organizations. Understanding these limitations and being aware of them can help you make better decisions in your daily professional life.

Let's take a quick trip into the world of psychological research to understand why biases occur and how they can affect our behavior. According to the dual-process theory (Kahneman, 2011), our minds work with two cognitive systems to process information:

1. System 1 is fast, instinctive, and based on experiences, and therefore responsible for our *intuitive processing* (automatic).
2. System 2 is more thoughtful, rational, and based on consequences, which is why it regulates our *conscious reasoning* (controlled).

This theory explains that cognitive biases happen because our brain often relies on the fast, intuitive, and automatic system 1. This system quickly jumps to a conclusion based on limited information, even when a slower and more deliberate system 2 would be more appropriate. Although both systems are needed for effective decision-making, an imbalance or overreliance on one system can lead to errors. These errors can be poor decisions, bad judgments, or even mistakes.

Cognitive biases that often affect decision-makers:

Anchoring Bias

Studies have shown that people rely too heavily on the first piece of information encountered when making decisions, which affects their subsequent estimates and judgments. For example, if a company's initial market research suggests a high price point for a product, they may be biased toward setting a higher price even if subsequent research suggests a lower price would be more suitable.

Availability Bias

Our brain likes information that is easily accessible, much like a lot of us prefer the comfort of browsing through Netflix for a movie night rather than making the effort of researching every option, or even going to the cinema, to state just one of many everyday examples.[1] When making decisions, this convenience leads us to rely on information that is immediately present in our minds, such as recently heard news or past experiences that left a mark, which often leads to overestimating or misinterpreting the situation we're facing.

Confirmation Bias

The adage "You hear only what you want to hear" is an expression of confirmation bias. It's a familiar phenomenon: people gravitate toward information that aligns with their beliefs and they downplay or dismiss facts and evidence that challenge them. It's more common when issues are emotionally charged, or people have strong beliefs. Founders can easily fall into the trap of ignoring key market signals and misjudging what their customers really want, because their emotional investment in their business prevents them from dispassionately examining the facts (Von Bergen & Bressler, 2018, p. 6).

(*continued*)

[1]Netflix knows that they have only a brief window of 60–90 seconds for users to pick a new film before they leave the app. That's why they use advanced matching and machine learning techniques to keep users engaged and prevent them from losing interest (Cornell University, 2022).

(continued)

Hindsight Bias

If you've ever uttered the words "I knew it all along," you likely experienced hindsight bias. It describes the phenomenon when an unforeseen event becomes foreseeable in retrospect. Hindsight bias can also lead business professionals to believe that they can accurately predict future events, preventing them from learning from past experiences and leading to overconfidence in relying on familiar solutions instead of finding new ways to tackle familiar problems. Decision-makers in industries such as law, insurance, and finance – which all rely on accurate assessments of risk based on past events – can be particularly impacted by hindsight bias if it affects their objectivity.

Sunflower Bias

In the same way that sunflowers turn to the sun to survive, many managers in hierarchical organizations follow their superiors' beliefs and expectations instead of using their own expertise. This behavior shows unequal power dynamics, where employees are more likely to keep quiet about their own opinions to protect their careers (Boot et al., 2005, p. 501). For one thing, it weakens the value of delegating tasks, because the company spends resources to gather information, while the employees ignore this information to follow their bosses' beliefs (Boot et al., 2005, p. 502). Secondly, if occurring on a broader scale throughout the organization, it can lead to critical decision-making, stifling innovation and growth.

However, a study found that only 40% of managers know about cognitive bias and how to reduce it in decision-making (Muntwiler, 2021). The same study showed that 75% of these companies don't have any set methods to reduce biases in their decisions. Similarly, a survey by McKinsey showed that "reducing decision bias" was considered the most important goal for improving performance by nearly 800 board members and chairpersons (Baer et al., 2017).

The good news is that we *can* indeed learn to recognize and reduce some of our biases through training and special techniques (Croskerry, 2013). But we also want to get one thing straight from the start: changing one's thinking habits doesn't happen all at once. Cognitive debiasing is a journey, one that might never end. It takes a series of steps and a disciplined commitment, so unfortunately, a single management training course won't be enough. If you've read Kahneman's best-selling book *Thinking, Fast and Slow*, for example, you might have taken on a more skeptical view on adjusting personal thinking habits. The psychologist states that he is usually not hopeful about fixing biases (Kahneman, 2011).

Other researchers, however, are more optimistic about the idea that individuals are able to revise and correct biased decision-making – at least to some extent. We'll spare you the theoretical and empirical discussions of the last 40 years and provide a user-friendly and practical summary of the most commonly discussed strategies that you can apply individually.

There are two starting points to fix your brain's "bad habits." Help system 1 to make your first gut reactions better, for example, by changing your surroundings. In addition, help system 2 to strengthen your second thoughts, which check your gut reactions. This can be done by, for instance, taking your time and thinking things through. That being said, debiasing always involves a journey of reflection and intentional effort that, as research has shown, would typically involve these steps:

1. **Awareness of bias:** As a first step in the debiasing process, we need to become aware of our biases and the fact that they can influence our thoughts and behaviors.
2. **Motivation to change:** In this stage, individuals make the decision to actively work on reducing their biases.
3. **Initiation of change strategies:** This stage involves implementing specific techniques and strategies to reduce biases, such as mindfulness practices, debiasing exercises, and education.
4. **Maintenance of change:** Finally, this stage involves continuing to actively work on reducing biases, recognizing when biases arise, and using strategies to overcome them.

But what does this mean in the actual life of a company? The example of RWE, a large traditional electric utility, sparked our interest because the former CFO, Bernhard Günther, gave some insights in an interview on how they deal with confirmation bias in their daily work.

Example

How RWE Battles Cognitive Biases

The German electric utility RWE serves as a prime example of how even major industry players can recognize and modify their decision-making practices by acknowledging cognitive biases. Despite investing €10 billion in conventional power plants over a five-year period, the company misjudged the growth of green energy and advancements in renewable technology, as well as the shifting public opinion toward conventional power generation. In an effort to understand when and where RWE took a wrong turn, the company has initiated a comprehensive analysis of the decision-making dynamics that led to the misjudgments of the past years.

In addition to typical management issues like time and cost problems, and the unexpected Fukushima disaster, which caused the German government to quickly stop using nuclear power and speeded up the green energy transformation, RWE also found that they had fallen for some major cognitive biases. One reason for their decision was confirmation bias, which caused them to rely on the status quo and invest the entire €10 billion in a single opportunity within a short period, rather than stretching the period over a couple of years, which would have saved the company a majority of the overall sum. They also noticed that champion and sunflower biases were present, resulting in people below a certain rank not speaking up with their own opinions. For example, employees involved in investment evaluations felt that raising concerns about a promising investment from a different perspective could result in negative labeling.

On account of these findings and in response to an uncertain future for the energy industry, RWE initiated a cultural-change program with the arrival of their new CEO. The program was aimed at improving the management mindset and promoting mindfulness among employees. It also made it mandatory to list the debiasing techniques they used in any major proposal to the board. To further encourage conflict and dissent, the company also appointed a "devil's advocate" for big decisions, who would present the strongest negative case to create a constructive tension and improve decision-making in the long run across the whole organization.

(Günther, 2017)

We have seen in this chapter how to unlock the true potential of data-driven decision-making in your teams and company. The *4R framework* (Rhythm, Rigor, Reflection, Recovery) supports you (and Mike Tyson) when life happens while you are busy making plans. It guides you to assess the different parts, processes, routines, and activities of an organization.

Also, we dived into the needed upskilling as a crucial success factor and the pitfalls of biases. To round it out, we'll now talk about the last, very decisive puzzle piece: how to lead a DI organization.

CHAPTER

8

Leading a Decision Intelligence Organization

In this final chapter, we delve into the essential aspects of leading a DI organization. As we learned, the business landscape has become increasingly complex and competitive, and modern leaders face numerous challenges in navigating the uncertainty that comes with it. As a result, leaders are under pressure to make well-informed decisions and inspire and drive their teams to do the same. Our focus in this chapter is to explore the crucial role of leaders and distributed leadership in fostering an environment that maximizes decision quality, innovation, and adaptability within an organization.

Today's leaders can no longer rely solely on their knowledge and expertise to make critical decisions. In fact, when an organization is data-rich but finds itself stuck in a data-swamp, leaders must resist the temptation to make decisions in isolation. Instead, they need to lean into their teams, harnessing the collective intelligence, experience, and creativity that reside within them. Suppose leaders need to involve others in decision-making. In that case, they risk perpetuating a self-fulfilling prophecy. As a result, the organization remains trapped in a loop of poor decisions and stagnation despite the data they have.

This chapter will discuss the importance of recognizing and embracing the social processes that underpin decision-making and leadership within a DI organization. We will examine the critical interplay between *trust*, *courage*, *transparency*, and *experimentation* and how these elements create a thriving, innovative DI organization. Last but not least, we will delve into the role of leaders in one of the greatest challenges they may face: enabling *psychological safety*.

Trust and Courage

In our experience, we have seen that there is a range of actions a leader can take to build deep *trust* and inspire *courage*. These actions generate superior team engagement, cohesion, decision quality, and business and personal outcomes, laying the foundation for a DI organization. Furthermore, in our professional lives, we devote a significant portion of our waking hours to work, and everyone aspires to enjoy their time at the office while making valuable contributions through sound decision-making. Therefore, fostering trust and courage is paramount for a Decision Intelligence organization. We will start with biochemistry to underline the idea that trust and courage are more than soft and fluffy nice-to-have concepts. Afterward, we will deep-dive into the consequences of the social part in teams.

The Neuroscience of Trust: Unleashing Team Synergy through Oxytocin and Dopamine

When team members trust each other, there is greater likelihood that they will share information and collaborate effectively, even in the face of uncertainty or perceived threats. Logically, this results in better decision-making as team members leverage the collective knowledge and insights of the group. Neuroscientist Paul Zak's work on trust further supports the importance of fostering trust within teams. Zak found that trust is influenced by the release of oxytocin (Zak, 2012, p. 19).

So what is oxytocin? It's a hormone produced by the brain during social bonding, childbirth, and sexual activities. Sometimes referred to as the "love drug," oxytocin also has significant positive impact on our social, emotional, and cognitive behaviors. Elevated levels of oxytocin lead to reduced stress levels, enhanced comfort, relaxation, and a sense of loyalty toward others (Uvnäs-Moberg et al., 2019). And there's more good news: when oxytocin levels rise during social bonding, this contributes to developing loyalty among team members (De Dreu, 2012). In addition, research has shown that oxytocin is even released during stress and can buffer the adverse effects, thus promoting social bonding in times of adversity (Heinrichs et al., 2003). This relationship between stress and oxytocin emphasizes the importance of fostering resilience and trust among team members and highlights why team recovery is so important. In a nutshell, a positive connection with others creates higher oxytocin, reducing our stress levels significantly, which results in trusting each other. Everybody wins.

Now that we've looked at the biochemistry part, let's continue following the Decision Intelligence managerial path to driving trust and courage on a team, reflecting on an analytical deconstruction of what's happening in the trust and courage creation process.

When team members trust each other, it goes hand-in-hand with knowing each other's interpersonal nuances and professional and personal preferences, and even communication becomes easier because we are more forgiving of misunderstanding. As a result, each team member is more predictable to the others and no longer considered a threat. The social environment becomes more predictable, creating a safe space for each member to retreat and recover during challenging times.

This leads to higher-quality information sharing and collaboration toward solving challenges and achieving high-stakes goals. In addition, when team members experience deep trust with colleagues, this increases empathetic discourse. From a neuroscience perspective, empathetic discourse helps to maintain the health of the serotonergic reward pathway, which supports team members being able to self-soothe, rest, sleep, perform neuroplasticity, consolidate memories, manage emotions, and learn at a rapid rate. Empathetic discourse also helps team members to be connected both intellectually and emotionally.

This level of connection is crucial for reaching a state of *group flow*, a neurological phenomenon in which the team's brain chemistry is optimized for collaborative problem-solving and innovation. As Mihaly Csikszentmihalyi describes in his book *Flow: The Psychology of Optimal Experience*, flow is a state where "people are so involved in an activity that nothing else seems to matter; the experience itself is so enjoyable that people will do it even at great cost, for the sheer sake of doing it" (Csikszentmihalyi, 1990).

This ultimately creates more dopamine, a neurotransmitter released in the brain, which plays a significant role in shaping our behavior, mood, learning, and memory. Often referred to as the "happiness molecule," dopamine levels rise when we experience rewards, feel motivated, or engage in positive social interactions (Berridge & Robinson, 1998). These elevated dopamine levels contribute to happiness, promoting positive social interactions that facilitate relationship formation and social bonding (Depue & Morrone-Strupinsky, 2005). In building trust, the happiness generated by increased dopamine levels encourages positive social interactions, which fosters deep trust between individuals. When applied to a team setting, this concept of flow emphasizes the importance of fostering strong connections and trust among team members to unlock their collective problem-solving and innovative capabilities. So, in the end, we have mixed a cocktail of the "love drug" and the "happiness molecule," creating a team environment of trust with low stress and high flow.

The Power of Courage: Overcoming Fear and Uncertainty

Let's turn our focus to courage. Courage is the strength that empowers us to face fear, uncertainty, and adversity head on. It pushes us to take risks, embrace challenges, and make difficult decisions despite uncertain outcomes. As Simon Sinek would say, it's about "going out into the unknown and doing what's right, even when it's uncomfortable" (Sinek, 2014).

Consider a team facing a high-stakes decision with seemingly insurmountable challenges and risks. Courage enables them to move forward despite the odds, taking calculated risks and making tough choices, even when there's a chance of failure. Moreover, courage is critical to decision quality because it often fundamentally challenges existing paradigms, encouraging teams to reexamine the assumptions behind decisions or decision-making processes.

Courageous teams create conditions for individuals to dare to go beyond the usual incremental improvements and ask tough, fundamental questions about purpose, strategy, structure, and approach, despite what might be considered the group's "normal." In essence, courage is the driving force behind innovation and staying ahead of the curve. It is self-perpetuating, too. When teams bravely face significant challenges, they create an environment conducive to innovation and enhance the team's overall mental well-being, confidence, and resilience. This enhancement is attributed to the dopaminergic reward pathway, which regulates motivation and reinforcement (Ikemoto & Panksepp, 1999). By facing challenges head on and engaging in courageous actions, teams ultimately contribute to their ability to overcome adversity and drive innovation. The dopamine released when we face challenges and engage in courageous actions ultimately improves our ability to learn and stay motivated.

In our experience, even in a world where leaders and team members have access to the necessary data and information for making well-informed decisions, it's surprising how often they miss the perfect moment to act due to a lack of courage. Rather than boldly moving forward, they might continue to gather more data (even if sufficient data points have been researched and further data would generate disproportionate effort) or pass the responsibility on to others, resulting in no one stepping up to make the decision. This leads to decisions becoming obsolete as the context and flow of activities change – potentially resulting in the worst outcome: chaos and ambiguity take over, steering the course of events and preventing the organization from making effective decisions, ultimately demoralizing everyone involved.

Courage, therefore, is a vital ingredient for effective decision-making. Courageous leaders are those who encourage their teams to act boldly, understanding that setbacks are a possibility – and do the same themselves. As Nembhard and Edmondson's (2006) study suggests, courageous leadership is linked to higher levels of psychological safety within teams, leading to better decision-making. This emphasizes the significance of courage in creating a culture of trust and psychological safety at work. By embracing courage, leaders can empower their organizations to navigate uncertainty and thrive in the face of challenges (Nembhard & Edmondson, 2006).

When trust and courage come together, they forge a potent combination that fuels decision quality, experimentation, and innovation. Yet cultivating and sustaining trust and courage within an organization demands ongoing commitment, because these elements are fluid and can shift in response to new challenges and changing circumstances. It's essential to understand that achieving high trust and courage isn't a one-off triumph; it calls for continuous work to preserve and nurture these qualities amid constant change and adversity.

Transparency and Experimentation

Have you ever felt like an outsider in a group, unsure of what's happening because the information you need is hidden? It's not a great feeling and can hinder collaboration, trust, and effective decision-making within an organization. This is why *transparency* and *experimentation* are essential and where they come into play, forming a crucial duo in fostering a dynamic and innovative work environment.

The Force of Transparency: Fostering Trust, Belonging, and Informed Decision-Making

But first things first – what is transparency to begin with? Kaplan and Mikes (2012) define it as "the degree to which information is available to outsiders that enables them to have a true understanding of what is happening inside the organization" (Kaplan & Mikes, 2012). Notice the use of the word "outsiders" here. Transparency shapes the reality of inclusion and exclusion, determining whether or not someone feels like a group member. When transparency is present, it fosters a sense of belonging and shared understanding among insiders with access to the necessary information and knowledge for decision-making. Conversely, when transparency is lacking, it can create a sense of exclusion and disconnection for those not privy to relevant information. This perceived exclusion can make individuals feel like outsiders, potentially hampering collaboration, trust, and effective decision-making within the organization, creating stress and resistance.

Recall the relationship between being a team member, stress, trust, and the formula of "love drug plus happiness molecule." It's difficult to imagine that people in an organization lacking transparency would take on extreme ownership and accountability or make informed decisions if they don't feel a sense of belonging to the group and, ultimately, trust. It all comes back to transparency.

On the other hand, imagine a company where information is shared openly and consistently across all departments. Silos are broken down, and everyone can access the data they need for decision-making. This creates an environment where experimentation can flourish, leading to innovation and better decisions. However, we have felt experienced firsthand how brutal transparency can be misused, if not evolved responsibly. In his famous (and terrific) book *Good to Great*, Jim Collins and his team share the results of research about what distinguishes good from great organizations. They name transparency (while keeping faith in the long-term success) as one of the key factors to succeed: "Retain faith that you will prevail in the end, regardless of the difficulties AND at the same time confront the most brutal facts of your current reality, whatever they might be" (Collins, 2001). The citation from Collins's work highlights transparency's crucial role in ensuring organizational success. It demonstrates that when applied responsibly, transparency can help organizations face their challenges head on while maintaining an unwavering belief in their ultimate success. This balance between transparency and faith in long-term success is vital for fostering a healthy, productive, innovative organizational culture.

Implementing transparency can be like a magician revealing a trick – once the secret is exposed, the magic disappears, and the performance can never be the same again. Achieving the right level of transparency in an organization requires intention, commitment, and time to evolve as people. Educating and empowering employees to handle the information and data they receive responsibly is essential, ensuring that transparency fosters growth and improvement rather than hindering progress, creating fear within the system, or turning it into a blame game. Striking the right balance is crucial to avoid the extremes of sharing too much or too little information. Organizations can create a thriving and well-informed environment that promotes curiosity and innovation while preserving the magic of collaborative success by providing everyone with access to the information necessary for making decisions in their respective areas of responsibility. For leaders, mastering the art of managing transparency is a vital skill, much like a magician maintaining the perfect balance between revealing and concealing to contribute to their organization's long-term success.

Transparency lays the groundwork for a successful DI organization, and with that foundation in place, it's time to shift our focus to another critical component: experimentation.

Embracing Experimentation: The Key to Innovation and Adaptability in DI Organizations

Experimentation is "the process of conducting controlled tests or investigations to discover new knowledge or validate existing theories" (Stefan & Jackson, 2008). In the context of an organization, it's about trying out new ideas, methods, or strategies, learning from them, and adapting as needed. It's like a chef continually experimenting with new ingredients and recipes to pursue culinary perfection. And, just as a chef might occasionally create a dish that tastes more like a science experiment gone south, organizations may encounter failures along the way.

A culinary masterpiece of experimentation is Noma, a renowned restaurant in Copenhagen. Noma's chef, René Redzepi, is famous for his innovative approach to cooking and dedication to using local ingredients. The restaurant is known for its unique and experimental dishes, some created through extensive trial and error. Redzepi and his team go to great lengths to forage for unusual ingredients and explore new combinations, pushing the boundaries of what is possible in the world of gastronomy. This daring approach to experimentation has led Noma to be recognized as one of the best restaurants in the world multiple times. The innovative system and avant-garde mindset shared by the entire kitchen team at Noma foster an exceptional atmosphere where anything seems possible. We asked the team about their experimentation failure rate during a one-day visit to the renowned restaurant. Surprisingly, they revealed that between 70% and 80% of their experiments don't succeed – experimenting is the norm for them. Yet, undeterred by these setbacks, they continue to learn and boldly venture into the unknown. As René Redzepi explains, "the test kitchen turns into a laboratory. It can take hundreds of tests to perfect a bean or walnut tofu – half a degree up and a little less salt can mean a world of difference. But from a single idea, an array of others can sprout" (Redzepi, Soberg, & Takahashi, 2022).

As Stefan and Jackson (2008) aptly put it, "experimentation is an essential process for organizations that want to stay ahead of the competition and adapt to the ever-changing business environment" (Stefan & Jackson, 2008). This statement highlights experimentation's vital role in rapidly gathering ideas from a network of contributors, maintaining agility in testing these ideas, and fostering innovation within an organization.

Now let's connect the dots between transparency and experimentation. In an organization that embraces transparency, information flows freely and consistently across all departments. As a result, employees can access the data they need for decision-making, empowering them to try new ideas, learn from their mistakes, and contribute to the organization's growth and success. It's like having the ultimate cookbook, where everyone can see the recipes, learn from each other's experiences, and add their unique flavor to the mix – just like Noma's kitchen's creative and collaborative atmosphere.

Experimentation demands courage, because it involves embracing risk and the possibility of failure. When employees feel supported by a transparent and trusting environment, they're more inclined to take these risks, knowing they have the backing of their teammates and leaders. After all, it's easier to laugh together at a shared "kitchen disaster" when you know you're all in it together, striving for something better.

In summary, transparency and experimentation are indispensable elements of a DI organization. Organizations can inspire employees to take calculated risks, innovate, and make better decisions by cultivating a culture of idea-sharing, openness, and experimentation. This powerful synergy between transparency and experiment sets the stage for a dynamic and adaptive organization poised for ongoing growth, success, and being avant-garde, such as seen with the team at Noma.

Psychological Safety: The Secret Ingredient for a Decision Intelligence Organization

Trust and courage, transparency and experimentation share a common theme – all of these are collective processes. Nurtured within groups of people, they have an incredible potential to lead to powerful new ideas. Yet, as with any collective process, without the right conditions, what started with the best intentions can create long-lasting damage to organizations. Therefore, a key ingredient is needed to underpin the culture of trust, courage, transparency, and experimentation: psychological safety.

What Is Psychological Safety?

Psychological safety is a critical component in the success and performance of teams. It allows team members to take risks without fear of reprisal, just like the chefs at Noma experimenting with bold new flavors and techniques.

Let's examine two definitions from prominent expert Amy Edmondson to better understand this concept. In her book *The Fearless Organization*, Edmondson defines psychological safety as "the belief that one will not be punished or humiliated for speaking up with ideas, questions, concerns, or mistakes" (Edmondson, 2018). Edmondson's earlier definition of psychological safety highlights a similar idea. She describes it as "a shared belief held by team members that the team is safe for interpersonal risk-taking" (Edmondson, 1999). Both definitions emphasize a sense of support for expressing new or challenging thoughts and opinions with others without fear.

Just by considering the definition of psychological safety, one might assume it to be synonymous with security that leaders provide for their teams, shielding them from the external pressures. Once achieved, a state of comfort is a key attribute of the team working environment, shared by all and effortlessly acquired by new joiners. On the other hand, creating psychological safety is hard work that is shared by the whole team through engaging in conscious and painstaking practice of reflection, feedback, and refinement of how they work together. Much like climate, psychological safety is sensitive to any shifts within and outside the team context, such as changes to the team composition or the broader organizational strategy. Unless the team continuously examines the impact of these events and the team's response to them, psychological safety is difficult to maintain.

When team members feel safe to share their thoughts and perspectives, they can collaborate more effectively and make better decisions. Team members are more likely to take risks, challenge the status quo, and engage in constructive conflict, all of which can lead to better decision-making and improved team performance (Edmondson, 1999; Edmondson & Lei, 2014). This is particularly important in situations with limited time and resources and where the consequences of a bad decision can be significant. However, decision-making is often complicated, particularly in team settings where diverse perspectives and opinions are at play. When team members do not feel psychologically safe, they may hold back their ideas and opinions, leading to missed opportunities and suboptimal decisions. Fear of negative consequences can also result in conformity and groupthink, which can hinder diversity of thinking and outcomes.

Example

Improved Team Performance in Software Development

In the early 2000s, Google's People Operations department set out to identify what makes their most effective teams so successful. After analyzing data from over 200 teams, they found that the most successful teams were those with high levels of psychological safety (Duhigg, 2016). One example of a team with high psychological safety was a group of engineers who worked on the Google Maps application. The team was made up of individuals from different departments, with diverse backgrounds and skill sets. Despite their differences, they worked together seamlessly, with team members freely sharing their thoughts and ideas without fear of negative consequences. In fact, team members were encouraged to challenge each other and to speak up if they disagreed with an idea. This culture of psychological safety led to better decision-making, higher levels of innovation, and improved team performance. The team was able to quickly identify and address issues, make decisions more efficiently, and develop new features that met the needs of their users (Duhigg, 2016).

Making intelligent decisions in a timely and effective manner is essential for achieving business objectives and maintaining a competitive edge. As a result, many organizations have embraced psychological safety as a key element of team collaboration and decision-making. NASA 4D leadership development program, created after the Space Shuttle *Challenger* disaster, recognized the critical role of social dynamics and relationships in people's ability to speak up to raise challenges and concerns (Pellerin, n.d). The Defense Advanced Research Projects Agency's (DARPA) approach to fostering risk-taking and tolerance to failure as an essential driver of innovation is similarly grounded in psychological safety within and across teams (DARPA, 2016). For Novartis, psychological safety has been built into the fabric of R&D to ensure safe and innovative outcomes for patients (Novartis, n.d.).

Example

Netflix's Culture of Decision-Making

Netflix's unique corporate culture has been a subject of interest for many years due to its emphasis on individual responsibility and decision-making. The company's approach to decision-making, known as "context, not control," has been a driving force behind its success. By avoiding micromanagement and hierarchical structures, Netflix empowers its employees to make decisions based on their own expertise and the context of the situation.

This approach has been instrumental in the company's ability to innovate and stay ahead of the competition. For instance, when Netflix decided to shift from a DVD rental service to a streaming platform, it was a decision made by a small team of employees, without input from senior management. This decision ended up being a game-changer for the company and revolutionized the entertainment industry as a whole. In her very readable book *Powerful*, former Netflix chief talent officer Patty

McCord explains that the company's focus is on results rather than process. This means that employees are encouraged to make quick, efficient decisions that prioritize outcomes over bureaucracy (McCord, 2017).

For example, if a customer is having a problem with their account, an employee is free to offer a refund or another solution without seeking approval from their manager. This allows for faster, more personalized service that puts the customer's needs first. However, this approach also requires a high degree of trust and psychological safety. To empower employees to make important decisions, Netflix must create an environment where individuals feel safe to express their ideas and concerns. This includes a culture of transparency, where information is shared freely across departments and levels of the organization.

Additionally, the company encourages constructive conflict, where employees are free to debate ideas and challenge assumptions, leading to more informed decisions. Netflix's unique approach to decision-making has played a critical role in its success. By prioritizing individual responsibility and results over process, the company has been able to stay agile and innovative in an ever-changing market.

Psychological safety is a critical enabler of decision intelligence in team settings. Leaders must establish a culture of trust and respect by encouraging constructive feedback and promoting an atmosphere where all team members feel valued and heard. All team members must play an active role in promoting and maintaining psychological safety, and individual and team-level factors such as personality traits, job characteristics, and work design must be taken into account to create a more psychologically safe environment.

Pathway to Enhanced Decision Intelligence: Psychological Safety Meets the 4R Framework

Our experience has shown that psychological safety can be both a proxy and an enabler for intelligent decision-making. Based on our experience across industries and geographies, we have compiled best practice for how leaders can apply the above mentioned 4Rs framework (Rhythm, Rigor, Reflection, and Recovery) to psychological safety. By concentrating on these four vital elements, organizations can minimize the threat of losing trust and courage, ensuring a thriving environment that promotes innovation, resiliency, and effective decision-making.

The following best-practices are designed to be a starting point for leaders and we encourage them not just to adopt these approaches, but evolve and define their own ideas.

1. **Rhythm and psychological safety – harmonizing team dynamics for enhanced decision intelligence:** Rhythm ensures the heartbeat, stability, structure, and clarity, which is corrected and protected by psychological safety. Teams who regularly measure and reflect on their psychological safety levels outperform those that don't (Duhigg, 2016, pp. 95–96).

   In previous chapters, we discussed the positive impact of DI on KPIs. Now, we introduce the concept of key development indicators (KDIs) to focus on progress and growth. KDIs are distinct from KPIs because they focus on the development and growth of teams and individuals rather than on performance outcomes. By paying attention to KDIs, teams can better understand their strengths and weaknesses, allowing them to strike a balance between performance and growth.

   As a rule of thumb, we recommend that teams establish a rhythm of measuring psychological safety every three to four weeks and openly discuss the results in a safe space. It's essential to remember that KDIs are not used for performance management or talent discussions. We want honest conversations, not artificially inflated numbers that don't reflect reality.

2. **Rigor and psychological safety – strengthening trust and precision in decision-making:** Rigor enables leaders to drive psychological safety by creating high standards, holding oneself and others accountable, and committing to decisions once they are taken. Some of the most successful teams that we have worked with established the rigor of making psychological safety an ongoing, long-term priority that is codified in a team's values and ways of working. Establishing psychological safety takes time and commitment to establish and needs to be actively maintained – especially in light of how quickly psychological safety can drop with simply a word or phrase from a leader.

   An additional best practice for leveraging rigor to establish psychological safety is enabling an environment where people can disagree constructively but ultimately commit to a decision. The ability to disagree during the decision-making process – and allowing for radical candor – helps ensure all perspectives are heard, creates a clear norm around when and why it is useful to have conflict, and avoids groupthink. Sticking with decisions once they are made enables teams and organizations to learn from their decisions and observe valuable lessons from the impacts of their decisions over time.

3. **Reflection and psychological safety – the power of introspection:** As we continue this exploration, let us first acknowledge the power of reflection. When leaders take a step back and engage in introspection, they can better understand their emotions, motivations, and biases. By doing so, they can avoid impulsive or reactive behaviors that may hinder progress.

Similarly, teams can benefit immensely from regular reflections and retrospectives conducted in a psychologically safe environment. These sessions can help identify conflicts, proactively manage challenges, and prevent blockers from escalating and negatively impacting a team's decision-making abilities.

Retrospectives have long been a core practice for agile teams, helping them optimize their ways of working, improve team effectiveness, and develop a learning and growth mindset. However, non-agile teams can also reap the rewards of regular reflection in a safe space. Through our experience of working with over 200 projects across diverse teams and industries, we've found that retrospectives are most successful when they do the following:

- Start with objective, confidential, and real-time data on psychological safety
- Are facilitated by a neutral third party who acts independently in the best interest of all team members
- Empower each member of the team to commit to one to three actions and/or new behaviors on what they will improve

An additional best practice is to assess levels of psychological safety anonymously either during or immediately after a group has taken a decision and enable the team and the leader to understand their levels of psychological safety in a high-stakes context of decision-making. In our experience, teams that are following these best practices uncover their blind spots and biases, and ultimately make more inclusive decisions.

4. **Recovery and psychological safety – enhancing resilience and thriving in adversity:** The ability to take time to rest

and recharge is essential for creating psychological safety. When people are overworked, stressed, or burned out, they are less likely to feel safe speaking up or taking risks. By encouraging their team members to take time off, prioritize self-care, and avoid overworking, leaders can create an environment where everyone feels supported and valued, which can contribute to a sense of psychological safety.

Our experience has shown that teams who build short periods of recovery into their planning, in which workloads are temporarily and intentionally reduced, can sustain higher levels of performance over longer periods of time.

To actively foster a sense of psychological safety, individuals and teams also need to be aware of their cognitive loads and build in small recovery moments into daily routines to free up the cognitive capacity. The cognitive load theory – developed in 1988 by John Sweller, professor emeritus at the University of South Wales, Sydney – states that our brain's working memory is only able to hold small amounts of information at a time. When team members feel psychologically safe, they are spending less cognitive capacity on worrying about team dynamics and can focus more on the task or decision at hand.

By following these best practices, leaders can establish a psychologically safe environment that fosters improved decision-making outcomes and enables teams to consider diverse perspectives, assess risks and benefits, and make inclusive decisions.

Embracing Failure and Forging Forward

In the pursuit of success, there will be times when your decisions will falter despite your best efforts. You've followed every step, analyzed the data, reflected on biases, and engaged your team.

However, the outcome is different from what you expected. These moments can make you feel isolated and disheartened as a leader or decision-maker.

So, how do you handle this situation? How do you embrace failure and forge forward?

First and foremost, take ownership of the situation. Then recognize that responsibility ultimately lies with you as a leader or decision-maker. This mindset empowers you to acknowledge failure, learn from it, and take decisive action to correct the course. Instead of shying away from responsibility, face it head on and demonstrate to your team that you're committed to making things right.

Remember, it's crucial to maintain open and honest communication with your team. Share the lessons learned from the failed decision and encourage them to provide feedback on the process. By fostering a culture of trust and transparency, you'll strengthen your team's resilience and ensure everyone is aligned and moving forward together.

Resilience is essential for navigating adversity. As a leader, your attitude and determination set the tone for your team. Embrace the challenge and demonstrate that setbacks are an opportunity to grow and return stronger. Show your team that you are committed to learning, adapting, and driving forward, and they will follow your example.

Finally, remember to practice self-compassion. As a leader, you're not immune to the impact of failure. Allow yourself the space to process the experience and remember that no one is perfect. By treating yourself with kindness and understanding, you'll be better equipped to support your team and continue leading with confidence.

As Albert Einstein once said, "A person who never made a mistake never tried anything new." By taking ownership, focusing on critical areas for improvement, maintaining open communication, demonstrating resilience, and practicing self-compassion, you'll overcome setbacks and strengthen your leadership and decision-making capabilities. Embrace failure, learn from it, and lead your team to greater heights in the realm of decision intelligence.

Epilogue

As we look to the future of decision-making, we can imagine a world where humans and machines work together seamlessly to make complex choices and solve intricate problems. In this future, artificial intelligence and machine learning algorithms will have become even more advanced, capable of processing vast amounts of data and offering insights and recommendations that were previously impossible. However, while machines may be able to provide valuable input and analysis, humans will still play a crucial role in the decision-making process, bringing their own unique perspectives, creativity, and emotional intelligence to the table.

The ethical and moral considerations of decision-making will also continue to be of paramount importance. As we confront increasingly complex and pressing global challenges, from climate change to social inequality, the need for thoughtful, responsible decision-making will only become more acute. It will be essential for decision-makers to balance the interests of different stakeholders, manage interdependencies, and consider the long-term consequences of their actions. In a nutshell: embrace complexity!

We are deeply convinced that, to survive, companies of tomorrow must transform into organizations where the DNA is

Decision Intelligence. With the right tools, skills, and mindset, we can create a world where decision-making is a force for positive change and progress, a world where the challenges we face are met with wisdom, creativity, and empathy.

What was a story in a science fiction book yesterday will be reality in the future. Just as it was shocking 25 years ago to see an AI defeat the grandmaster at chess, today we see the first 100% AI agents living together in a small town and "wake up, cook breakfast, and head to work; artists paint, while authors write," and they even start to go to a Valentine's date (Park et al., 2023).

As we stand on the doorstep of this future, we are filled with a sense of awe and wonder. What kind of world will we create with our decisions? Will we use our newfound knowledge and technology to better the lives of all beings on this planet, or will we succumb to our base instincts and continue down a path of destruction and chaos? The power to shape our future is in our hands, but we must be mindful of the historical context that has brought us to this point. We stand on the shoulders of giants, from the ancient philosophers who first pondered the mysteries of decision-making, to the modern-day pioneers who have unlocked the secrets of the human mind. Anthropology, psychology, sociology, and other fields have given us invaluable insights into the complex processes that govern our decision-making. We now know that our choices are influenced by a myriad of factors, from our emotions and biases to our social and cultural context. As we peer into the future, we must also confront the challenges that lie ahead. The world is changing at an unprecedented pace, with new technologies and global challenges shaping the way we live and make decisions.

Yet, despite these challenges, we remain hopeful. We believe that by embracing our past and learning from our mistakes, we can forge a brighter future for ourselves and for generations to come. We have the power to shape our destiny, to choose a path that leads us forward.

The future of decision-making is in our hands. Let us choose wisely.

References

ADAC. (2023). "Autonomes Fahren: So fahren wir in Zukunft." Accessed January 4, 2023. https://www.adac.de/rund-ums-fahrzeug/ausstattung-technik-zubehoer/autonomes-fahren/technik-vernetzung/aktuelle-technik/

Adams, Douglas. (1979). *The Hitchhiker's Guide to the Galaxy*. Pan Books.

Alberti, Marco. (2022). "How do you manage a company holistically?" Translated by the authors; min 11:13. Accessed April 13, 2023. https://www.youtube.com/watch?v=7Zk1WpKxQZY

Aminov, Iskander, Aaron De Smet, Gregor Jost, & David Mendelsohn. (2019). "Decision making in the age of urgency." McKinsey & Company, April 30. https://www.mckinsey.com/capabilities/people-and-organizational-performance/our-insights/decision-making-in-the-age-of-urgency

Baer, Tobias, Sven Heiligtag, & Hamid Samandari. (2017). "The business logic in debiasing." McKinsey & Company, May 23. https://www.mckinsey.com/capabilities/risk-and-resilience/our-insights/the-business-logic-in-debiasing

Baker, Pam. (2022). *Decision Intelligence for Dummies*. Hoboken, NJ: John Wiley & Sons.

Berridge, K. C., & T. E. Robinson. (1998). What is the role of dopamine in reward: hedonic impact, reward learning, or incentive salience? *Brain Research Reviews* 28(3): 309–369.

Blanchard, Kenneth H., & Sheldon Bowles. (2011). *Gung Ho! How to Motivate People in Any Organization*, 2nd ed. New York: William Morrow; Dublin: HarperCollins.

Boot, W. A. Arnoud, Todd T. Milbourn, & Anjan V. Thakor. (2005). Sunflower management and capital budgeting. *Journal of Business* 78(2): 501–527. https://www.jstor.org/stable/10.1086/427636

Brandstetter, Thomas. (2021). "Nicht ohne Grund!" Max-Planck-Gesellschaft, October 4. https://www.mpg.de/17651253/ki-kausalitaet

Burkhardt, Christoph. (2018). *Don't Be a Robot: Seven Survival Strategies in the Age of Artificial Intelligence*. Midas Management, 219.

Cagan, Marty. (2018). *Inspired: How to Create Tech Products Customers Love*. Hoboken, NJ: Wiley.

Collins, Jim. (2001). *Good to Great: Why Some Companies Make the Leap . . . and Others Don't*. New York: HarperCollins, p. 86.

Cornell University. (2022). "How Netflix Uses Matching to Pick the Best Thumbnail for You." Accessed April 7, 2023. https://blogs.cornell.edu/info2040/2022/09/28/how-netflix-uses-matching-to-pick-the-best-thumbnail-for-you/

Croskerry, Pat, Geeta Singhal, & Sílvia Mamede. (2013). Cognitive debiasing 1: origins of bias and theory of debiasing. *BMJ Quality & Safety* 22: ii58–ii64, https://qualitysafety.bmj.com/content/22/Suppl_2/ii58, and "Cognitive debiasing 2: impediments to and strategies for change," ii65–ii72, https://qualitysafety.bmj.com/content/22/Suppl_2/ii65

Csikszentmihalyi, M. (1990). *Flow: The Psychology of Optimal Experience*. Harper & Row, p. 4.

DARPA (Defense Advanced Research Projects Agency). (2016). "Innovation at DARPA." https://www.darpa.mil/attachments/DARPA_Innovation_2016.pdf

Dastin, Jeffrey. (2018). "Amazon scraps secret AI recruiting tool that showed bias against women." *Reuters*. October 11. Accessed April 16, 2023. https://www.reuters.com/article/us-amazon-com-jobs-automation-insight-idUSKCN1MK08G

Davenport, T. H., & J. G. Harris (2007). *Competing on Analytics: The New Science of Winning*. Cambridge, MA: Harvard Business School Press.

Deb, Kalyanmoy, Amrit Pratap, Sameer Agarwal, & T.A.M.T. Meyarivan. (2002). A fast and elitist multiobjective genetic algorithm: NSGA-II. IEEE Transactions on Evolutionary Computation 6(2): 182–197, doi:10.1109/4235.996017

Decosmo, Joe. (2018). "Why You Should Take a Decision-First Approach to Analytics." *Forbes*, October 17. https://www.forbes.com/sites/forbestechcouncil/2018/10/17/why-you-should-take-a-decision-first-approach-to-analytics/?sh=4fdad5462e19

De Dreu, C. K. (2012). Oxytocin modulates cooperation within and competition between groups: an integrative review and research agenda. *Hormones and Behavior* 61(3): 419–428.

Depue, R. A., & J. V. Morrone-Strupinsky. (2005). A neurobehavioral model of affiliative bonding: implications for conceptualizing a human trait of affiliation. *Behavioral and Brain Sciences* 28(3): 313–350.

Doshi-Velez, Finale, & Been Kim. (2017). "Towards a Rigorous Science of Interpretable Machine Learning." arXiv preprint arXiv:1702.08608

Duhigg, Charles. (2016). *Smarter Faster Better: The Secrets of Being Productive in Life and Business*. New York: Random House.

Edmondson, A. C. (1999). Psychological safety and learning behavior in work teams. *Administrative Science Quarterly* 44(2): 350–383.

Edmondson, A. C. (2018). *The Fearless Organization: Creating Psychological Safety in the Workplace for Learning, Innovation, and Growth*. Hoboken, NJ: John Wiley & Sons.

Edmondson, A. C., & Z. Lei. (2014). Psychological safety: The history, renaissance, and future of an interpersonal construct. *Annual Review of Organizational Psychology and Organizational Behavior* 1: 23–43.

Eisenhardt, K. M. (1989). Building theories from case study research. *Academy of Management Review* 14(4): 532–550.

Freeman, R. E. (2010). *Strategic Management: A Stakeholder Approach*. New York: Cambridge University Press.

Gigerenzer, G., & Selten, R. (Eds.). (2002). *Bounded Rationality: The Adaptive Toolbox*. Cambridge, MA: MIT Press.

Graham, Chris. (2016). "Crowd turns its back on Hillary Clinton as photo captures the age of the selfie," *Telegraph*, September 26. Accessed April 11, 2023. https://www.telegraph.co.uk/news/2016/09/25/crowd-turns-its-back-on-hillary-clinton-as-photo-captures-the-ag/

Günther, Bernhard. (2017). "A Case Study in Combating Bias." Interview by Sven Heiligtag and Allen Webb. McKinsey Quarterly, May 11. https://www.mckinsey.com/capabilities/people-and-organizational-performance/our-insights/a-case-study-in-combating-bias

Harrison, J. S., & A. C. Wicks. (2015). Stakeholder theory, value, and firm performance. *Business Ethics Quarterly* 25(2): 207–237.

Heinrichs, M., T. Baumgartner, C. Kirschbaum, & U. Ehlert. (2003). Social support and oxytocin interact to suppress cortisol and subjective responses to psychosocial stress. *Biological Psychiatry* 54(12): 1389–1398.

Ikemoto, S., & J. Panksepp. (1999). The role of the nucleus accumbens dopamine in motivated behavior: a unifying interpretation with special reference to reward-seeking. *Brain Research Reviews* 31(1): 6–41.

Kahneman, D. (2011). *Thinking, Fast and Slow*. New York: Farrar, Straus and Giroux.

Kahneman, D., & A. Tversky. (1974). Judgment under uncertainty: heuristics and biases. *Science* 185(4157): 1124–1131.

Kahneman, Daniel, & Amos Tversky. (1979). Prospect theory: an analysis of decision under risk. *Econometrica* 47(2): 263–292. https://doi.org/10.2307/1914185

Kaplan, Robert S., & Anette Mikes. (2012). Managing risks: a new framework. *Harvard Business Review* 90(6): 48–60.

Khandani, Amir E., Adlar J. Kim, & Andrew W. Lo. (2010). Consumer credit-risk models via machine-learning algorithms. *Journal of Banking & Finance* 34(11): 2767–2787, November.

Kim, Gene, Kevin Behr, & George Spafford. (2013). *The Phoenix Project: A Novel about IT, DevOps, and Helping Your Business Win*. Portland, OR: IT Revolution Press, pp. 43–70.

Kolb, David A. (1984). *Experiential Learning: Experience as the Source of Learning and Development*. Englewood Cliffs, NJ: Prentice Hall.

Kruse, Peter. (2008). "How do people react to growing complexity ?" Translated by the authors. Accessed April 8, 2023. https://www.youtube.com/watch?v=m3QqDOeSahU

Kulkarni, Rohit. (2019). "Big Data Goes Big." *Forbes*. February 7, 2019. https://www.forbes.com/sites/rkulkarni/2019/02/07/big-data-goes-big/?sh=89dd2320d7b4

Larson, Erik. (2021). "How to Use the Decision-Back Approach to Elevate Insights and Analytics?" *Forbes*, December 15. https://www.forbes.com/sites/eriklarson/2022/05/10/gartners-decision-intelligence-trend-is-taking-off-what-took-so-long/?sh=7a2003384e68

Leong, Lester. (2019). "How Data Science Makes Money – for Businesses." June 17. https://towardsdatascience.com/how-data-science-makes-money-for-businesses-203daba010c1

Li, Y., Z. Li, & L. Zhang. (2017), Human vs. machine: A comparison study of conventional and machine learning approaches for credit scoring. *Journal of Risk and Financial Management* 10(2): 10. https://doi.org/10.3390/jrfm10020010

Madsbjerg, Christian. (2017). *Sensemaking: The Power of the Humanities in the Age of the Algorithm*. Hachette UK.

Madsbjerg, Christian, & Mikkel Rasmussen. (2014). "How Lego took to anthropology." *Financial Times*, March 9. Accessed April 16, 2023. https://www.ft.com/content/b071990c-9d4c-11e3-a599-00144feab7de

March, J. G., & H. A. Simon. (1958). *Organizations*. New York: John Wiley & Sons.

MarketsandMarkets. (2023). "Decision Intelligence Market." Accessed April 8, 2023. https://www.marketsandmarkets.com/Market-Reports/decision-intelligence-market-11498239.html

Marler, R. Timothy, & Jasbir S. Arora. (2004). Survey of multi-objective optimization methods for engineering. *Structural and Multidisciplinary Optimization* 26: 369–395.

McCord, Patty. (2017). *Powerful: Building a Culture of Freedom and Responsibility*. New York: Silicon Guild.

McKinsey, Niko Mohr, & Holger Hürtgen. (2018). "Achieving business impact with data: A comprehensive perspective on the insights value chain," April. https://www.mckinsey.com/~/media/mckinsey/business%20functions/mckinsey%20analytics/our%20insights/achieving%20business%20impact%20with%20data/achieving-business-impact-with-data_final.ashx

Mitchell, T. M., R. Caruana, D. Freitag, J. McDermott, & D. Zabowski. (1994). "Humans and Machines: A Multidimensional Comparison." *AAAI-94 Proceedings of the Twelfth National Conference on Artificial Intelligence* 1: 964–971. https://www.aaai.org/Library/National-Conferences/1994/aaai94-137.php

Moreno, Hugo. (2017). "Data Analytics Is No Longer a Nice Option: It's the Core of the Enterprise." *Forbes*, June 12. Accessed April 16, 2023. https://www.forbes.com/sites/forbesinsights/2017/06/12/data-analytics-is-no-longer-a-nice-option-its-the-core-of-the-enterprise/?sh=351e3a1677ec

Muntwiler, J. (2021). The role of cognitive biases in managerial decision making: the case of German companies. *Journal of Business and Management Sciences* 9(1): 1–10.

Nembhard, I. M., & A. C. Edmondson. (2006). Making it safe: the effects of leader inclusiveness and professional status on psychological safety and improvement efforts in health care teams. *Journal of Organizational Behavior* 27(7): 941–966.

Nemeth, C. J., & Kwan, J. L. (1987). Minority influence, divergent thinking and detection of correct solutions. *Journal of Applied Social Psychology* 17(9): 788–799. https://doi.org/10.1111/j.1559-1816.1987.tb00339.x

Novartis. (n.d.) "Psychological Safety." Accessed April 17, 2023. https://www.health.novartis.co.uk/formulary-and-service-support/partnership/psychological-safety/#id25241

Nutt, P.C. (2008). Investigating the success of decision making processes. *Journal of Management Studies* 45, 425–455. https://doi.org/10.1111/j.1467-6486.2007.00756.x

Palm, H., F. Rang, F. Mueller, & M. Guerster. (2021). "Multiobjective Design Optimization of Hybrid Electric Rail Vehicle Powertrains." *IEEE International Symposium on Systems Engineering (ISSE)*, Vienna, Austria.

Park, Joon Sung, Joseph C. O'Brien, Carrie J. Cai, Meredith Ringel Morris, Percy Liang, & Michael S. Bernstein. (2023). Generative agents: Interactive simulacra of human behavior. https://doi.org/10.48550/arXiv.2304.03442

Pearl, J., & D. & Mackenzie. (2019). *The Book of Why: The New Science of Cause and Effect*. Penguin Books, p. 33.

Pellerin, Charlie. (n.d.) "NASA 4D Leadership Development Program." Accessed April 17, 2023. https://www.nasa.gov/pdf/293252main_62680main_charlie_pellerin_forum7.pdf

Petrović, Đorđe, Radomir Mijailović, & Dalibor Pešić. (2020). "Traffic Accidents with Autonomous Vehicles: Type of Collisions, Manoeuvres and Errors of Conventional Vehicles' Drivers." *Transportation Research Procedia*, 45: 161–168. https://www.sciencedirect.com/science/article/pii/S2352146520301654

Prahalad, C. K., & G. Hamel. (1994). *Competing for the Future*. Cambridge, MA: Harvard Business School Press.

Pratt, Lorien. (2019). *Link: How Decision Intelligence Connects Data, Actions, and Outcomes*. Emerald Publishing.

Provost, F., & T. Fawcett (2013). Data science and its relationship to big data and data-driven decision making. *Big Data* 1, 51–59. https://doi.org/10.1089/big.2013.1508

Raelin, J. D., & C. G. Cataldo. (2011). Whither middle management? Empowering interface and the failure of organizational change. *Journal of Change Management* 11(4): 481–507. doi: 10.1080/14697017.2011.630509

Rang, Fabian Rang. (2021). "Optimization Geeks: Multi-Objective Optimization: Easy explanation what it is and why you should use it!" https://www.youtube.com/watch?v=Zchm_W6tFz4&list=PLFBydIvdkgImvl8YlPRXYg1jcJC89puOj&index=1, Min 6:36

Redzepi, René, Mette Søberg, & Junichi Takahashi. (2022). *NOMA 2.0. Vegetable, Forest, Ocean*. Workman Publishing.

Rock, D. (2008). SCARF: A brain-based model for collaborating with and influencing others. *Neuroleadership Journal* 1, 1–9.

Rollings, Mike. (2021). "How to Make Better Business Decisions." Gartner, October 20. https://www.gartner.com/smarterwithgartner/how-to-make-better-business-decisions

Rudin, C. (2019). "The Interpretability of Machine Learning: A View from the Human Sciences." arXiv preprint arXiv:1911.02508. https://arxiv.org/abs/1911.02508

Saller, Thomas, Thomas Mauder, & Gerhard Flesch. (2016). "Das 1x1 des Unternehmertums: Von der Unternehmensgründung bis zur erfolgreichen Führung." Wiesbaden: Springer Gabler.

Silver, D., et al. (2016). Mastering the game of go with deep neural networks and tree search. *Nature* 529, no. 7587 (2016): 484–489. doi:10.1038/nature16961

Sinek, S. (2014). *Leaders Eat Last: Why Some Teams Pull Together and Others Don't*. Penguin, p. 21.

Smith, Ralph C. (2014). *Uncertainty Quantification: Theory, Implementation, and Applications*. Vol. 12, Computational Science and Engineering Series . Siam.

Snowden, D. J., & M. E. Boone. (2007). A leader's framework for decision making. *Harvard Business Review* 85(11): 68–76. Accessed April 10, 2023. https://hbr.org/2007/11/a-leaders-framework-for-decision-making

Statista. (2021). Volume of data/information created, captured, copied, and consumed worldwide from 2010 to 2020, with forecasts from 2021 to 2025. Accessed June 5, 2023. https://www.statista.com/statistics/871513/worldwide-data-created/

Stefan, Thomas, & Paul Jackson. (2008). *The Art of Experimentation: Unlocking the Potential of Innovation*. New York: Random House, p. 134.

Suwa, M., & B. Tversky. (2002). *External Representations Contribute to the Dynamic Construction of Ideas*. Springer, pp. 341–343.

Sweller, John. (1988). Cognitive load during problem solving: Effects on learning. *Cognitive Science* 12(2): 257–285.

Taleb, Nassim Nicholas. (2007). *The Black Swan: The Impact of the Highly Improbable*. New York: Random House.

Taleb, Nassim Nicholas. (2012). *Antifragile: Things That Gain from Disorder*. New York: Random House.

Uvnäs-Moberg, K., M. Petersson, & H. Olausson. (2019). Affective and social neuroscience approaches to understanding oxytocin function and pharmacology. *Trends in Cognitive Sciences* 23(9): 782–796.

Vandevelde, Pieter-Jan. (2021). "How to Use Data to Make Your Business More Profitable." 4psquare, April 1. https://4psquare.com/blog/profitable-business-by-data/

Von Bergen, C., & Martin Bressler. (2018). Cognitive biases in decision making. *Journal of Leadership, Accountability and Ethics* 15(1): 1–11.

Zak, Paul J. (2012). *The Moral Molecule: The Source of Love and Prosperity*. New York: Dutton.

Zak, P. J. (2017). The neuroscience of trust. *Harvard Business Review* 95(1): 84–90.

Zheng, M., J. K. Marsh, J. V. Nickerson, et al. (2020). How causal information affects decisions. *Cognitive Research* 5(6). https://doi.org/10.1186/s41235-020-0206-z

Additional Resources

Argyris, C. (1998). Empowerment: the emperor's new clothes. *Harvard Business Review* 76(3): 98–105.

Ariely, D. (2008). *Predictably Irrational: The Hidden Forces That Shape Our Decisions*. HarperCollins.

Baer, M., & M. Frese. (2003). Innovation is not enough: Climates for initiative and psychological safety, process innovations, and firm performance. *Journal of Organizational Behavior* 24(1): 45–68.

Banich, Marie T., & Rebecca J. Compton. (2018). *Cognitive Neuroscience*, 4th ed. Cambridge University Press.

Bardwick, J. M. (1991). *Empowerment in Organizations: How to Spark Exceptional Performance*. Hoboken, NJ: John Wiley & Sons.

Bateman, T. S., & J. M. Crant. (1993). The proactive component of organizational behavior: A measure and correlates. *Journal of Organizational Behavior* 14(2), 103–118. https://doi.org/10.1002/job.4030140202

Bazerman, M. H., & D. A. Moore. (2013). *Judgment in Managerial Decision Making*. Hoboken, NJ: John Wiley & Sons.

Bigley, G. A., & K. H. Roberts. (2001). The incident command system: High-reliability organizing for complex and volatile task environments. *Academy of Management Journal* 44(6): 1281–1299.

Blanchard, K., J. P. Carlos, & A. Randolph. (1996). *Empowerment Takes More Than a Minute*. Berrett-Koehler Publishers.

Block, P. (1991). *The Empowered Manager: Positive Political Skills at Work*. Hoboken, NJ: John Wiley & Sons.

Bonabeau, E., N. Bodick, & C. Armstrong. (2018). Decision intelligence. *Harvard Business Review* 96(1): 64–71.

Carter, C. S. (1998). Neuroendocrine perspectives on social attachment and love. *Psychoneuroendocrinology* 23(8): 779–818.

Carter, N. M. (1998). "An integration of three theories of motivation and performance: Goal setting, self-efficacy, and reinforcement theory." Unpublished doctoral dissertation, University of Maryland, College Park.

Cooperrider, D. L., S. Srivastva, & F. J. Barrett. (2019). "Fearless: How Safety and Trust Can Help Financial Services Thrive Even During Disruption and Transformational Change." Weatherhead School of Management at Case Western Reserve University.

Coyle, D. (2018). *The Culture Code: The Secrets of Highly Successful Groups*. Bantam Books.

Decision Intelligence Lab. "Why do we see unpredictable events as predictable after they occur?" Accessed February 6, 2023. https://thedecisionlab.com/biases/hindsight-bias

Deephouse, D. L., W. J. Lawler, & K. Workman. (2008). The power of empowerment: What the best companies do to help their employees succeed. *Organizational Dynamics* 37(3): 237–245.

Diamond, Jared. (1999). *Guns, Germs, and Steel: The Fates of Human Societies.* W. W. Norton & Company.

Epstein, D. (2019). *Range: Why Generalists Triumph in a Specialized World.* Riverhead Books.

Gallup. (2020). "State of the American Workplace Report." https://www.gallup.com/workplace/285818/state-american-workplace-report.aspx

Gorman, A. (2017). Leadership for exploration and discovery. *Space Policy* 41: 12–19.

Hammond, J. S., R. L. Keeney, & H. Raiffa. (2006). *Smart Choices: A Practical Guide to Making Better Decisions.* Broadway Business.

Janis, I. L., & L. Mann. (1977). *Decision Making: A Psychological Analysis of Conflict, Choice, and Commitment.* Free Press.

Keeney, R. L., & H. Raiffa. (1976). *Decision-making with Multiple Objectives: Preferences and Value Tradeoffs.* John Wiley & Sons.

Keeney, R. L., & H. Raiffa. (1993). *Decisions with Multiple Objectives: Preferences and Value Tradeoffs*, 2nd ed. Cambridge, UK: Cambridge University Press.

Kirschner, P. A., J. Sweller, & R. E. Clark. (2006). Why minimal guidance during instruction does not work: an analysis of the failure of constructivist, discovery, problem-based, experiential, and inquiry-based teaching. *Educational Psychologist* 41(2): 75–86.

Knight, F. H. (1921). *Risk, Uncertainty, and Profit.* Boston, MA: Houghton Mifflin.

Kotler, S. 2021. *The Art of Impossible: A Peak Performance Primer.* Harper Wave.

Kozlowski, S. W., & B. S. Bell. (2013). "Work Groups and Teams in Organizations." *Handbook of Psychology*, 2nd ed., pp. 412–440. Hoboken, NJ: John Wiley & Sons.

Kruse, Peter. (2008). "nextpractice: Erfolgreiches Management von Instabilität. Veränderung durch Vernetzung." Offenbach: GABAL Verlag.

Kunsch, P. L., & J. Springael. (2015). *Multiple Criteria Decision Analysis: Applications in Environment and Health.* CRC Press.

Landucci, L., & F. Lamperti. (2020). A pandemic of cognitive bias. *Nature Human Behaviour* 4(5): 447–450. https://doi.org/10.1007/s00134-020-06293-y

Larson, Erik. (2022). "Gartner's Decision Intelligence Trend Is Taking Off. What Took So Long?" *Forbes*, May 10, 2022. https://www.forbes.com/sites/eriklarson/2022/05/10/gartners-decision-intelligence-trend-is-taking-off-what-took-so-long/?sh=7a2003384e68

Li, J., Y. Li, & X. Zhang. (2017). Fintech and credit risk management: Evidence from China. *Journal of Financial Stability*, 29: 21–33.

Lipshitz, R., G. Klein, J. Orasanu, & E. Salas. (Eds.). (2001). *Taking Stock of Naturalistic Decision Making*. Springer Science & Business Media.

March, J. G. (1994). *A Primer on Decision Making: How Decisions Happen*. Free Press.

Mayer, R. C., & M. B. Gavin. (2005). Trust in management and performance: Who minds the shop while the employees watch the boss? *Academy of Management Journal* 48(5): 874–888. https://doi.org/10.5465/amj.2005.18803927

McEwen, B. S. (2017). Allostasis and the epigenetics of brain and body health over the life course: the brain on stress. *Journal of the American Medical Association Psychiatry* 74(6): 551–552.

Muntwiler, Christian. (2021). "Debiasing management decisions: Overcoming the practice/theory gap within the managerial decision process." Take Conference 2021, University St. Gallen. https://www.alexandria.unisg.ch/263136/

Newman, A., R. Donohue, & N. Eva. (2017). Psychological safety: a systematic review of the literature. *Human Resource Management Review* 27(3): 521–535.

Pellegrini, E. K., & T. A. Scandura. (2008). Leader–member exchange (LMX), differentiation, and psychological safety: A multilevel examination. *Leadership Quarterly*, 19(2): 179–194.

Rimmele, U., K. Hediger, M. Heinrichs, & P. Klaver. (2009). Oxytocin makes a face in memory familiar. *Journal of Neuroscience* 29(1): 38–42.

Rosenholtz, R., J. Huang, & K. A. Ehinger. (2005). Rethinking the role of top-down attention in vision: effects attributable to a lossy representation in peripheral vision. *Advances in Neural Information Processing Systems*: 1139–1146.

Rosenholtz, R., J. Li, J. Mansfield, & Z. Jin. (2005). Human and machine perception of contextual information in scene recognition. *ACM Transactions on Applied Perception* 2(3): 203–222. https://doi.org/10.1145/1095872.1095875

Rudin, C. (2019). Stop explaining black box machine learning models for high stakes decisions and use interpretable models instead. *Nature Machine Intelligence* 1(5): 206–215. doi: 10.1038/s42256-019-0048-x

Simon, H. A. (1955). A behavioral model of rational choice. *Quarterly Journal of Economics* 69(1): 99–118.

Simon, H. A. (1957). *Models of Man: Social and Rational.* New York: John Wiley & Sons.

Stern, A., & D. Grinspoon. (2018). *The New Horizons Pluto Mission: An Insider's Look at the Triumphs and Challenges*. Smithsonian Books.

Tegmark, M. (2017). *Life 3.0: Being Human in the Age of Artificial Intelligence.* New York: Knopf.

Von Bergen, Clarence, & Martin Bressler. (2018). Confirmation bias in entrepreneurship. *Journal of Management Policy and Practice* 19(3): 74–84. https://www.researchgate.net/publication/327823193_Confirmation_Bias_in_Entrepreneurship

Wheatley, M. J. (2006). *Leadership and the New Science: Discovering Order in a Chaotic World.* Berrett-Koehler Publishers.

Wise, R. A. (2004). Dopamine, learning and motivation. *Nature Reviews Neuroscience* 5(6): 483–494.

Yue, L., et al. (2018). "Auto-Detection of Alzheimer's disease using deep convolutional neural networks." International Conference on Natural Computation, Fuzzy Systems and Knowledge Discovery, doi: 10.1109/FSKD.2018.8687207

Index

B

C

P